Personality Development

Complete Guide for Personality Development

(A Guide to Living With and Managing Paranoid Personality Disorder)

Evelyn Malone

Published By **Jordan Levy**

Evelyn Malone

Personality Development: Complete Guide for Personality Development (A Guide to Living With and Managing Paranoid Personality Disorder)

ISBN   978-1-998901-15-9

No part of this guidebook shall be reproduced in any form without permission in writing from the publisher except in the case of brief quotations embodied in critical articles or reviews.

Legal & Disclaimer

The information contained in this ebook is not designed to replace or take the place of any form of medicine or professional medical advice. The information in this ebook has been provided for educational & entertainment purposes only.

The information contained in this book has been compiled from sources deemed reliable, and it is accurate to the best of the Author's knowledge; however, the Author cannot guarantee its accuracy and validity and cannot be held liable for any errors or omissions. Changes are periodically made to this book. You must consult your doctor or get professional medical advice before using any of the suggested remedies, techniques, or information in this book.

Table Of Contents

Chapter 1: Relationship Building: Self-Confidence & Personality

Self-confidence is the greatest force to attract success. This is one quality that will bring the outside world to your feet, both professionally as well as personally. A common extension to self-confidence is charisma. Charisma doesn't refer to self-confidence. Instead, it's a close corollary which adds more power.

What is Self-Confidence?

Self-confidence means having faith in one's capabilities. Each personality has three parts:

* Your perception of yourself.

* What others think of your character.

* What others think of you.

Your personality can be formed when all three of these aspects are merged. Self-confidence refers only to that which focuses on aspect number 1. You'll find that the opinions of others about you are not a problem if you believe in your abilities and yourself. Don't let other peoples' reactions influence your life.

The Roots Behind Self-Confidence

Confident people are not born. If the early years focus on positive aspects, justice and tolerance for errors, the child will become confident. If, on the other side, the early experiences were negative and focused on punishments and harsh criticism, the child would grow into a confused adult who would have low self-esteem.

One example is that a person with high self confidence would think, "I need learn from my mistakes." This is important to ensure that next time I get better marks." However, a person with low selfconfidence would think "Oh, it was only a normal thing." I am hopeless. "I am completely stupid and useless."

Why is Self-Confidence Essential?

Self-confidence is crucial because it is the main factor that attracts success. It is that voice in your head that says, "I can."

Without it, we would be restricted in all areas of our lives. Low self-confidence would most often result in many negative traits which would further hamper a person's basic abilities. It would also create a vicious cycle of self-defeat. Low self-confidence is not a factor that will allow people to move forward. It would make it difficult for them to overcome past mistakes and encourage growth.

How do you build your self-confidence and self-esteem?

Three steps are necessary to help you build self-confidence. These three steps can help you grow your self-confidence and make it a powerful guiding force to achieve success in both professional and personal life.

Step No. 1. Preparations- This is the first step to building self-confidence. It is important to prepare your mind before you begin working on your self confidence. If your mind isn't focused and committed to this end, nothing can be accomplished.

1. Take note of all your accomplishments. This is the first task you need to complete. How far have you come in your journey. Write down all the achievements that you have to date and place them in a visible location where you can easily see them every day. This is the list of all your successes so far. This is the starting point.

2. Identify Your Strength And Weaknesses - run a quick SWOT (Strengths-Weaknesses-Opportunities-Threats) analysis on yourself. You should pay attention to all four aspects. But, you should focus on your strengths.

3. Set Goals - goals act as destination points. Without one, you will never reach anywhere. Setting clear goals is essential for building self-confidence. The goal of your life is not something you need to decide right away. You'll have the time to do that later. Instead, create goals that you can achieve in six months, one-year,

or five years. Break down your goals further into smaller goals and celebrate every step you take. Your self-confidence is bound to grow with each achievement.

4. The key to success is in your mind. You may have heard the phrase, "If You think you can do it, you can" or "If You think you cannot, you won't". You must work hard to get your mind set in a positive direction. Be able to identify negative self-deprecating beliefs and replace them by positive, encouraging thoughts. Your mind should always be focused on the "I can", mode.

5. Commit Yourself to Success - It won't be easy to reach the level of self-confidence that will become a powerful, magnetic force within your life. It is crucial that you commit to yourself that your efforts will not falter until you reach the desired level. You need to build your will power and persevere regardless of what happens.

Step No. Step 2. The Journey. This is the beginning of the longest journey, but only one small step. After making a decision, you need to move. These are the steps you need to take in order to get there.

1. Fill the Gaps. Use your knowledge and abilities to remove as many weaknesses as possible. You can look at the goals you've set and the strengths, and weaknesses, that you've identified in SWOT. Fill in the gaps as quickly as possible.

2. Take it one step at the time. The whole thing can sometimes seem daunting and overwhelming. If paralysis is threatening, don't look at the big picture. Be patient and take each step one at a while, celebrating every little thing along the route. After some time, you'll realize the journey isn't as difficult as it seemed at the start and it will get easier.

3. You Can Set Your Mind on Finding The Treasure. Think of this as a journey to discover an important treasure. The Force of Self-Confidence is a treasure that will bring you all the things you

desire in life. Therefore, to get there, train you mind to "treasuremap" the journey. Every achievement should be a milestone towards your treasure. Imagine your success.

Step No. Step 3. Picking Up Speed - As your journey continues, your self confidence will grow each time you reach a goal. Gradually, your self-confidence will increase, so you can believe in yourself and in your ability to achieve your goals. You will be thirstier for success as you go.

This is very good. The goal should be to increase speed and move towards the final destination. However, it is important to be cautious not to become too confident or arrogant. Keep grounded, SWOT-analyzing yourself regularly and maintaining a healthy amount of self-doubt as well as overconfidence.

How do you use the Force?

Now you can build self-confidence and charisma. This is your chance to make a difference in your life. Your ability to attract people and your self-confidence will make you more attractive and help you have better relationships. Charisma is one the most desirable traits that you could develop. With it you can literally conquer all of the world.

Do you need more proof of your charisma and self-confidence to prove it? You only need to look at some of history's most influential and successful people - Oprah. Mohammad Ali. Winston Churchill. George Clooney. Napoleon Bonaparte.

What is it that these towering personalities share in common? These individuals were/are able get others to do the things they desire. They were able get people to trust, follow and admire them, even though they may not share their ideology. This is The Force's power.

The Force Could Change Your Life Forever

Now that you have it you need to learn how to make it work for you. The Force is available to:

Increase your persuasion power - self-confidence comes from inner passion, strong beliefs or convictions. People will respond to you with enthusiasm when you make them do something you want.

*Become a leader. Napoleon had started his army career in the lower grades. His charisma and unstoppable self-confidence helped him rise through the ranks to become an imperial. You'll find charismatic leaders are respected by everyone you know. People gravitate to The Force, which makes them more likely to obey. This is one pillar of The Force.

* Inspire other people - The Force is going to inspire you. The majority of people who come into contact with you will find that you are attractive, interesting and fascinating. Everywhere you go, you'll find people who want to surround you with them, be there for

you and do whatever it takes to please you.

* Increase your friends circle - The Force will help you attract more friends. You can spread a positive and confident aura around others that will attract them like iron fillings magnets. The Force can help you make friends that are genuine and close.

* You are successful: If you find someone with charisma or self-confidence, you know you've found a successful person. "Success," here, isn't just about professional accomplishment. It also includes personal relationships. Charismatic people are often successful in both professional as well as personal life. They are able balance the worlds and have the ability to enjoy both to the fullest.

* Be true happiness - The Force will bring you happiness. Charismatic, self-confident individuals are passionate. They can identify and pursue their passions. They will follow whatever

passions they have, regardless of whether or not other people believe in them. It is this passion they find success with; it is this passion their life will be filled with happiness.

How to use the Force to improve your professional and personal lives

Being confident and charismatic is an instinctive trait that will allow you to know what to do in any given situation. You may still be learning the basics of how to use this newly acquired Force in your life. Here are some helpful tips:

* Walk the walk - You must live by the principles of The Force. Your passion should shine through in all you do. You should have passion in everything you do, in your professional and personal relationships.

* Do not choose the limelight. Charismatic people can seem bigger than life simply by choosing to stay in the limelight. They try to be there for everyone, good and bad. They inspire by

their example. They are always there to assist when they are required. They are seen. They are outgoing. They get along well with people and enjoy their company.

* It doesn't matter if you're silent - charismatic people who are self-confident and confident are excellent listeners. They are also good communicators. They continually send signals through body language and eye contacts. An imitating gesture, a firm handshake and a warm smile can all be used to communicate loudly, clearly, even when the person is not talking.

Push beyond the reasonable - As the old saying goes, "Nothing Great was Ever Attained by a Reasonable Man." You will find success when you put yourself and others in a position to go beyond the "possible". It is not the right place for you if you are always challenging yourself and everyone else to achieve the best outcome.

* Use The Spotlight technique - The person who has The Force is aware that to conquer people one needs to touch the heart as much as the mind. It is no surprise that charismatic people form such fulfilling relationships with everyone who they meet. The spotlight technique requires that you focus on the person speaking to you and give your 100% unblinking attention. It is simple. Focus on the person you are speaking to and give them your complete attention.

This would improve your relationship with your family and friends and inspire them to admire and love you. The spotlight effect must be perfected by:

* Place your 100% focus on the person

* Eye contact is essential at all times

* Always keep a warm expression in your face

* Get the other person to talk

Mirror the person's expressions and voice tone.

When you use The Force correctly, you can change your entire life. You will be able to make every decision and do everything a success. Although it may be difficult to use The Force for what you want initially, you will be able eventually to reach your goals with just a little bit of practice and perseverance.

Chapter 2: How To Influence Others Using The Force

What is Charisma, and how can it be defined? Charisma can be described as the inherent magnetism a person has that draws others to him/her. The terms "charisma" synonyms include captivating, seductive.

Is charisma a natural trait or can it be learned and nurtured? It is both. There are people born with it. And there are others who learn it to fully harness its power. Here are the five top characteristics that you must develop in order to experience the power and charisma.

1. You must be confident and self-confident. Being charismatic requires you to be your best self. Being self-confident means being comfortable with yourself, full of passion, happy with your identity, and optimistic. It may seem like a long list. But, if you pay attention, each factor is a fallout.

2. You should be an excellent communicator - charismatic people share great stories. Listening to what they have to say is like hearing it in your mind. Why? Because they speak with such conviction. They speak with such conviction that you can see they are certain about what they are saying. They are aware and up-to-date with their surroundings, facts and other people. They are always well-informed and can instill trust through their words. Charismatics are known for being able to communicate clearly.

3. Learning and understanding body language is crucial. It can help you speak louder and more clearly without actually saying anything. You have to appear as though you own the universe. As the absolute monarch of the world, your body changes as a result.

You're filled with self-confidence. Who would dare challenge you, if you were the king of the world? See how your body changes when it feels in control. Fake it until the magnetic power you have through your body language is evident.

4. The conversation is always about you. Close your eyes. Think about what you love most about charismatic friends. You will find the first thing that pops into your head is, "I can be open with this person like none other." "I can talk on any topic"

This is because charisma is about making people feel comfortable and at ease around you. This will make people feel comfortable around you. Charismatic people will make you feel like the only one in the conversation.

5. You must be an excellent listener. This is the key ingredient to a great relationship. Learn to listen. Pay attention to what the other person has to say. Listen with intense attention. Engage with empathy.

6. You need to develop or have a sense humor. A charismatic individual will use humor just as Santa Claus uses gifts. He makes people laugh at their circumstances and themselves. Humor is a unique way to make people feel at home, to make them happy and to be able to communicate with them.

Why is It Important? How does it complement The Force of Self Conscience?

Charisma, or Charisma, is crucial because it's easy to lose self-confidence and become excessively confident. Overconfidence is not the key to success. Instead, it can cause you to fail.

Charisma is the ingredient to help you maintain the balance between too little or too much confidence. To reach the world and grab what you want, nurture The Force from within. If self confidence is the main ingredient in The Force, then charisma will make it complete.

This is why those we love will have charisma and self confidence. This is why it is so important to have both charisma and self-confidence.

People who have The Force can also influence others. It is like magic. When people speak, they listen with passion, are motivated with the same purpose, and are willing even to sacrifice their lives for others.

The Force could be used to influence people in many ways, including Napoleon Bonaparte's, Hitler, Abraham Lincoln and Mahatma Buddha. Each of the above cases showed that someone had The Force, and used it to get people to move the way they desired.

* Mahatma Buddha led the non-violent campaign against the British. He was followed by millions of Indians, who were often beaten, jailed or even killed.

* Napoleon Bonaparte led his soldiers through some of most dangerous terrains.

* Abraham Lincoln was in a position to abolish slavery, and hold the American nations together despite the disastrous civil war.

* Hitler unites Germans against other "inferiors."

These are just some of the many people who used their Force over time. There are many other people who use their Force every day. It doesn't always have to be on a historic level or on a great individual, though most Force members will naturally rise in visibility and leadership.

To achieve their dreams, leaders know they need to have the support of others. This will require them to be able to influence other people to do their bidding with full will, goodwill, and conviction. Learn to use The Force in order to influence others at such high levels.

It is important to remember that The Force can only be used to draw people to you. If you don't use The Force for the greater good of society and are moving in positive directions, The Force will fail. This is an example of Hitler or Abraham Lincoln.

Hitler united Germany to fight all "inferior" races. His beliefs influenced the German people so much that they agreed with his plan to destroy the Jews. The Force was unable to control people because of its inhumanity. Hitler committed suicide at his death; otherwise, he'd have been executed.

Abraham Lincoln opposed the abolishment of slavery. It was a violently opposed change that has cost millions of innocent lives. Abraham Lincoln was, however, one of the most beloved and loved Presidents in the United States.

How can the Force be used to influence others?

The Force doesn't have to be reserved for elite leaders. The Force can be used by everyone to inspire, draw, or influence others to do what they want. The Force can be used to successfully pass a job interview. The Force can be used for getting your children to listen to what you have to say (this may well be the best reason to learn The Force).

The Force's power can be applied in all areas of your lives to make things happen faster and win people over. It will allow you to make friends, attract new business partners, gain popularity in your own family, and increase your visibility wherever you go.

Do you wish to leverage The Force's influence and power to attract people? Here's what you could do:

* Do your research and learn as much as you can about the subject. Being able to speak with authority requires that you are well versed in the subject. The Force cannot be used if you're not prepared 200%.

* Remain in control of the situation. People gravitate to people who show

self-assurance, are calm and cool in any situation. This is accomplished by projecting inner-calm (even when you are in complete panic), self reliance, and self confidence.

* Exude warmth. Nothing will draw people more than warmth. To truly care for others, you must feel connected to them and empathize with their feelings. People respond to warmth and will lift up towards you.

* Your mouth and body should communicate the same language. It is possible to say great things that will attract and influence others. But if your body language speaks differently, you won't be able to hold them on for long. You must learn how to project a confident and powerful image through your body language.

* Listen carefully to what others have to say. The Force is most effective when you master the art. Listening is vital. You can create a special relationship with anyone you meet when you master this

art. In other words, everyone you meet will become a fan of yours.

* Exude Positive Energy - You would have discovered that certain people can get you motivated and happy just by being there. These are the people who can use The Force and radiate positive energies around others. Enthusiasm, passion, determination and enthusiasm are key to success. Positive energy, enthusiasm and passion are all things that attract others.

* Be open-minded to new ideas and viewpoints - it is essential to be open to innovative ideas, new perspectives, new angles, new ways of looking at the world, etc. People will always find people who are interested or curious about new things.

* Be humble. The Force cannot attract or influence people like you unless you are humble. Humility is what helps to keep the ego in check, and it makes charismatic people feel more connected with others. No matter how rich or famous they become, great people will

always be humble and connected back to their roots.

* Have a smiling smile. It's a common saying that charismatic people will have a smiling, pleasant face. If you have a sourpussy look, will you be attracted to them or willing to talk/ listen to them? A smiling face attracts people closer because it is non-threatening, reassuring, and can help them feel more comfortable.

* Display high adaptive power - charismatic, self-confident people will be able easily to adapt to changes in their lives without losing their senses. This ability will inspire trust, admiration, and win people's hearts and minds.

* Very high in emotional intelligence. You can use The Force for your emotions to be in touch and freely express them. People will connect easily to those who aren't afraid to show that they are human. Feeling in touch with yourself would allow you to recognize the feelings

of others and help you connect with them.

* Be friendly to the eyes. Charism and self-confidence are equally important. You should always look impeccable and be well groomed. This shows that you care about what other people think about you. It lets others know that you are in charge and instills confidence in yourself. Einstein was an example of this. However, he was extremely intelligent and lacked The Force. He was always dressed in a dirty look which didn't draw too many people to his side.

Chapter 3: Body Language And The Force

Self confidence can be described and emulated easily; charisma is more difficult to convey. This is an attribute that sometimes defies established boundaries. How do we define attractiveness? How do you define magnetism, for example? How do we define the quality of being alluring? It's not easy to describe it because even though these words/ expressions conjure vivid visuals, words are never enough to explain them.

The Force is the person with self-confidence and charisma. They are able to use body language to motivate, inspire, trust and motivate those around them. They can do this by using many traits of their personality, and most importantly by complementing their body with the image they wish to project.

Body language and the leader image you want to project

The Force is looking for a charismatic leader who is self-confident and charismatic. Your body language is an important part of your professional and personal image.

You must be able read and understand body language in order to attract people and keep them interested.

How can you harness the power of The Force with body language?

There are many elements you must learn and master about body language. Super leaders not only understand body language and how it can be used to their advantage, but are also able to interpret it.

1. "Why predator?" you might ask. The term predator here refers to the highest power, i.e. It signifies that you are an Alpha and know everything. It is a sign that you are in control. It is meant both to scare you and to reassure you.

You may not know the steps of a ferocious predator when it is in your sight. It may be worthwhile to practice this walk before you go. This requires great self confidence.

You will be viewed as superior by others if you walk like this. The walk speaks louder than words.

2. Be patient and gracious. It's great to have your work completed quickly and efficiently. But, to make your body speak like a leader or at least a leader, you have to be aware of how slow you move. To do this, you must stand tall and remain confident. This picture is a combination that inspires trust.

Avoid making rapid, jerky movements. This shows that your are anxious about something. Instead, space out your movements so that you appear controlled and well-defined.

This will show that you are a capable and responsible person who is respected by all.

3. Always look people in a person's eyes. Shifty eyes can attract mistrust and

betrayal. While direct eye contact does the exact opposite, i.e. This builds trust and a sense of reliability. Many don't enjoy eye contact as it feels difficult or disrespectful. It's not true. People dislike it so much when the other person avoids eye contact. There's a way to ensure that it doesn't go off track.

Make eye contact, regardless of whether you're talking in a conversation with someone or in group settings. This should be done only occasionally, and not as a continuous stare. That would freak anybody. For eye contact to be established and maintained, you should scan the eyes of each pair that you wish to make contact with for about 1-2 secs. You can move on. Then, come back. The movement should feel fluid and smooth, to put it mildly.

4. You can put a smile on anyone's face, no matter how difficult or beautiful. Even if you're not currently experiencing any difficulties, a smiley could still lift your heart. It is very welcoming, reassuring as

well as pleasant to see someone smile genuinely at your face.

The smile is a key component of any leader, no matter how stressed they may be. A smile is a way to project trust and confidence. It also shows self-confidence.

5. Move with grace. Experts advise that great leaders should move with more grace. This is why it is so important to take dance classes and learn any type martial art you like.

You may be wondering what dance classes and martial arts have to do about charisma and self-confidence. Leaders who follow this routine experience a pleasant lightness on their feet, and improve their reflexes. Overall they appear confident, self-assured, prepared.

6. Your posture is key. It's what creates the first impression. You should stand straight with your shoulders pulled back. Make sure you take big, decisive steps. Your posture and movement, as well as the way your hands move, are all signs of

who you are.

It is obvious that your posture and power will determine how trustable you are to others.

7. Be calm and relaxed. The Providence will not let you down. It does not matter how terrible the circumstances, you need to be able and willing to stay calm, focused, and in control. Meditation is a practice that you can do if it is not something you are naturally capable of doing. It is not that difficult as you might think.

Your body language should demonstrate your ability stay calm. Every gesture that you make during any crisis will be noticed by many. This is because others will feel relieved and at ease knowing they can trust you.

How to Make People Like Yours Without Losing "You."

Everyone longs to be loved and valued. Sometimes the desire is so strong that you can become what others want. You will "lose" yourself when you do this. You can't be who you think you are.

People who do this have low self confidence and self-esteem. They feel not significant enough to count, so they tend to ignore their feelings or thoughts and follow the majority.

You don't need lose yourself to make people love you. People with The Force are charismatic, self-confident people who can make people like them without losing their identity. People who have high self esteem, confidence and charisma are more likely to inspire people to make changes and follow their lead.

Six top traits that make people want to be like you

You can make new friends without having to sacrifice your beliefs and feelings. Here's how self-confident people do this - and you too can.

1. Stop assuming power. You are self-confident and have high self esteem. There is no need to show your power stance anywhere, especially if people want to like you. You can be too straight, too rigid, or too formal if you have the "power attitude", which tells people that "I am better than" them.

Would you love to be treated like that? Yes, but not. This is why charismatic people abandon power and give all their importance to those they meet.

Meet someone you like. Take a step forward, not wait for them to approach you. This is the body language, which conveys "I am honored" and will make you a fan.

2. Nonsexual touching is great; touch people casually, lightly and without being too intrusive while greeting or talking to them. It is important to not do too much. Otherwise, you may come across as condescending, arrogant or worse, sexually agressive. A gentle pat on the back, or a quick touch on the shoulder

and upper arm make for a warm gesture. This makes you feel warm and real, which is what attracts people.

3. Talk to the other person about yourself - Have ever you had an encounter with someone with whom it was like a firework and you could tell him everything? It suddenly dawns on you that you really don't know anything about this person.

It takes only fifteen minutes to notice that you are in love with this person. But, it is not easy to know why. You discover that you like him as you feel comfortable telling him everything. He inspires trust and makes it easy to talk with him about your feelings, thoughts, or anything else.

How do you do that? This may seem simple, but it is not. How can you make the other person talk about you, but not about your own? How do they inspire this type of trust in others? Here's the way they do it.

* Listen intently to the person and pay attention as if they were the most important thing in all of existence. It is incredible how thrilling it is to know that you are being given 100% attention by the person you speak to.

Ask the right people the right questions. Without sounding intrusive, you want to learn as much about them as possible. It is important to ask the right kinds of questions. Open-ended questions can be more effective than a simple "yes or no" answer. Ask for examples such as "how did that happen", "how were you able to do it", or "when was it done". These questions should indicate that you are truly interested in what you're hearing and want to know more.

Appreciation is important to everyone. If you show genuine interest in others, people will find you magnetic.

* Share your weaknesses - nobody likes to be imperfect. Who doesn't love to be better than everyone? Who doesn't desire to be number one? This won't win

anyone any popularity contests. You need to demonstrate to others that your flaws are normal and that they can trust you.

People should not be approached as if they must win a competition. Let them win. People love people who are open-minded and accept others' abilities. People will attract you if they see you as vulnerable.

* There are no ulterior motives. Popular people are always available for help. They give their time with joy and sincerity - and ask nothing in return. Their efforts to help others are completely sincere and without ulterior motives.

People like friendly and helpful people. People like people who are genuinely interested in helping others. If you want people to love and be loved, then help them wherever they need. You will discover that people will not only be drawn to you but will go out of their ways to help when you need them.

* They leave you feeling good. Whenever it is time to go, the self-confident, charismatic person will make an indelible impact on the person he meets. A well-known person knows how close a conversation. As you leave, shake hands with your loved ones and say "I loved talking to" or "I am glad to have met you".

Refer to something that you learned while talking, such as: "I loved the manner you got through this interview. "I will use that method sometime." After you have finished, let him know you appreciate the interaction. This is the kind of appreciation we all love.

* Remember that we all have our problems. There isn't a single person on this planet who doesn't have troubles. But if you walk around with a long, gruff face and moping, it is easy to alienate others. People don't like gruff people.

Instead, keep smiling. Be happy and positive at all costs. Your positive attitude will radiate positivity wherever and whenever you go. People will gravitate towards your positive attitude, smiling face, and happy disposition.

* Laugh at yourself. There is nothing more endearing then to hear someone laugh about his mistakes. You don't need to be perfect, but it doesn't mean you shouldn't laugh at yourself. It will help others identify with your mistakes and inadequacies and therefore like you more.

Chapter 4: Making New Believers

Not all people have the ability to motivate others. Not everyone is able to motivate new followers or believers. To be able to do so, it takes practice, talent, and strength.

This is the charismatic characteristic of people who have The Force. They can attract people to themselves and turn them into new followers. Let us take a closer look at some prerequisites you need to be able to attract new believers.

1. Leaders should be taught. It is important to be perceived as someone who knows what he does and says. But you will quickly discover that not every leader makes an effort. Instead, he prefers to be a teacher. He teaches how things are done, which earns him the respect and belief of everyone.

You can foster creativity by being a teacher and encouraging others to reach their full potential. To get someone to believe in themselves, they need to believe you can make them better.

Encourage others to learn. Accept mistakes and learn from them.

2. You are a problem solving person - you know the saying "History will not remember who created the problems and who solved the problems". To attract new believers, you have to be a problem solutioner. People are at their most vulnerable when confronted with a problem. Leaders should show initiative and inspire others to seek solutions.

As a leader, you will be expected to find solutions or lead others to solve every problem or obstacle. This is not something you should do only once or twice in your lifetime. People will always look to you for help when they have problems. To do this, one must be:

* Creativity - there are no two problems alike, and no two solutions can be the exact same. Every problem should present itself in a creative way. You can use your experience as well as the knowledge of those around to come up with a solution.

* Ingenuity- Leaders need to think outside the boxes. It is important to use your imagination to find solutions to any problem quickly and efficiently. To put it another way, you should always be a step ahead of others.

* Effective - You must be highly efficient in order to lead others. You cannot have sincere intentions, work hard and earnest efforts without positive results. Therefore, you need to work hard and also find solutions.

* Analytical. You need to understand the problem in every detail and angle. Your vision must be sharper and more accurate than anyone else's. Your ability break down the problem and find solutions quickly would make it easier for you.

3. Visionaries are visionaries. Leaders are visionaries. All leaders are passionate about what is happening and have a greater vision that guides them. You are a visionary.

* Insightful Leaders have ingenious intuitions about everything that they do. This is due to the fact that they are extraordinarily tuned in to their intuition and allow themselves to be led by it. Each of us have gut feelings. Over time, however, we learn how to suppress them to the point where it is not discernible. You are a visionary.

* Be open-minded - not everything is what you think it is. There are many more details to the story than is apparent. As leader, it is important to recognize the subtleties and distinguish them. This requires an ability to observe with keenness.

* Big picture thinker - A visionary is able paint the larger picture so vividly that everyone who hears about it becomes reality. Only when others can see the big picture will they be motivated to take action in that direction. If the big picture is clear and appealing to the eyes and the heart, then there are new believers.

* Results-oriented. Every step must lead to the solution. To the bigger picture. A leader can inspire people to get results. A leader is focused, and always strives to achieve a goal that fits within the larger vision.

4. You are accountable. As a leader, it is your responsibility to be accountable. When things go wrong, you accept responsibility and are aware of your responsibilities. You are a leader accountable.

* Honesty: It is important that you are honest. People need to be able and willing to trust you with the rest of their lives. This is how new believers are made. Fair play, justice and honesty should guide all that you do and speak. All aspects of your daily life should reflect ethical principles, not just those at work.

* Transparent Leaders are a teacher and guru who have no secrets. All aspects of one's professional and personal lives can be seen and accessed by everyone. If a

leader is transparent in his actions, people begin to believe in him and feel safe following him.

* Lead by example. He is aware and willing to share his responsibilities with others. Leaders are able to inspire others and make them ethical, responsible, honest.

5. You are powerful - leaders can influence people's thoughts. You can change how they view the world and lead them towards the goal. You can get them to be:

* Motivational: As a leader, it is important to have strong motivational skills. You must be able and willing to inspire others to take a specific path that will lead them to their desired goals.

* An outstanding teacher - A leader is first and foremost a teacher. You need to be patient and compassionate.

* Encouraging -- A great leader would be able find something strong and worthy of

praise and inspire others to reach their full potential.

* Trustworthy- You cannot make people believe that you are genuine and trustworthy. To inspire trust, you must live up to your words.

* Humble - The greatest people are humble. This is because the wise realize how little they really know. Humility is the most attractive attribute of leaders. People are inspired to see humility in the life of a leader.

Attractiveness for both Persuasions and Personal Uses

People who have The Force exhibit a magnetism. They can persuade anyone to believe in them, follow them, and do what they ask. There is an attraction to these people that makes it easy for you to believe and do what they want. How are they able to do that? How do they convince people to do what it is they want? What is the secret to their persuasive powers?

A self-confident person can make persuasive speeches. These four steps are key to getting there.

Step 1: Learn the Basics

1. Timing is critical for persuasive speech. You must know when to say what, and this can be even more important than the way you say it. People are most vulnerable if they express gratitude for any assistance received. At that moment, they acknowledge you have helped them. When you ask them for a favor, they will likely refuse.

2. Establish a good relationship. This is true regardless of whether you are trying persuade just one person or all of them. People will be more open to hearing what you have to share and more likely do what they want.

Do your research. Get to know the people whom you are about to meet. If that is not possible engage with them and learn their likes. If that is not possible then you could establish your similarities based upon the overall situation. Perhaps you start with how hard the recess is hitting you. Instantly, your attention will be drawn to the situation and you will feel empathy for the majority.

3. Always use affirmation statements that are positive. This means you should only use positive statements when expressing your desires. To put it another way, "Don't neglect health" could be translated to "Take care" or "Don't let your health get in the way". Or "Don't tell a lie" can be better said as "Always speak the truth".

You are making a clear affirmative statement when you make it. This is an incredibly effective statement because the person will be able understand what your intentions are. They will then be able communicate clearly and in unambiguous terms your expectations.

4. Apply the Ethos–Pathos–Logos principles. Persuasion rests on three basic principles: credibility and emotion.

The person will be in your pocket when you press these three buttons.

* Credibility – people will respect those they consider trustworthy. Your words should be connected with high moral values and impeccable ethics. People like these aspects and want to be identified with them.

* Emotions: Use the emotion cards. They must feel what you have to say. Give them the opportunity to feel what you are saying and they will be able to do whatever you tell them.

* Logic is the most simple of all methods. You must convince someone - by using facts – that what they are saying makes sense.

5. In order to create the need, let us do XYZ. The listener will immediately ask "Why?" Then create the need. Tell them why this is important. Instill urgency in them about the necessity. You must act quickly, or tomorrow could be too late.

They should be required to act immediately.

Step 2: Perfect your skills

1. Rapid communication is key. Research indicates that people who speak fast tend to be more confident, intelligent, or knowledgeable. Develop a habit of speaking 160 to 190 words per minutes. You'll be able to persuade more people.

2. Master your body language. It is essential to be aware of the messages that your body sends to those around you. Mirror gestures could instantly draw another person to you. It is important to do this as gently as possible. Eye contact is important. Smile, hold your hands open and point your head towards the person. To put it another way, your body should reflect what is being said. "I'm interested in what you have to share."

3. Be patient, persistent, and keep following up. Find ways to follow up with the person and put your idea across without being too pushy. Persistence is a

great tool when it's used in the right way. There is a fine line between persistence, and being a bother. Don't let rejection get you down. Keep going. Abraham Lincoln is an excellent example for persistence that pays off.

Step 3: Identify the incentive

1. The economic incentiv - Everybody needs money. Then show them how you make profit, grow your business, and create income.

2. The social reward - In many cases, money is not an option. Make people feel that they are valued by their community and their children as well as their peers. You will make them want to eat out of your hands. This is often more powerful than the financial incentive. People want to be valued and acknowledged for their achievements.

3. The moral motivation - Sometimes people do not care that much about money and social image, but are motivated to view themselves as

examples for morals. The belief they can improve the world is what drives many people to action.

Step 4: Plan your Strategies

1. It is important to get them to agree to something. People are more consistent than they used to be. They will also be more likely to repeat what you've said if they do it again.

2. Show that you expect a lot. Expect a lot. Be open-minded, ask lots, seek the maximum, and be willing to give second and subsequent choices. People want you to keep your "high" image. If they fail to fulfill the first choice, then they will accept the second and third choices.

3. Reciprocity is a principle that you can give others something of high quality, and they will be compelled to reciprocate. The principle and practice of reciprocity are powerful. It's a common principle in business. The receiver will not only feel grateful that you gave him

something of value but also guilt for having done nothing.

Chapter 5: Using The Force To Build Your Business

All leaders must have self confidence. It is impossible to be a leader if you don't have confidence. This is what makes an individual a great leader. But, it is important to know the difference between a great leader and a unique leader. The latter type of leader has extraordinary self confidence and lots of charisma. This type leader is known as The Force.

How The Force Can Take Your Business From "Great", To "Dizzying Height"

The Force gives you the ability to do so much for your business, and to make it the best in its industry. Here are some tips to ensure your business is a success.

1. Take inspiration from your greatest achievements. All great leaders, great businessmen, great achievers, and all great leaders have had some failures. Failure is the only way to progress or achieve success. Each of these great leaders realized the importance of

learning from mistakes. Instead of being discouraged by failure, they chose not to dwell on it. They learned from it and were able to focus their energy on the highest achievements.

The Force employees choose to focus on the positive. This helps them feel more passion and drive to make their business grow without having to lose their stride.

Your self-confidence is what you need to become a great leader. You want to become a one-of-a kind leader. Put The Force to good work and view every failure and challenge in a positive light.

2. Get passionate about your work. With self-confidence, charisma, and confidence, you will be able to overcome any doubts regarding your ability. Being a leader is a great way to learn quickly that your luck will be proportional to the effort you put in. The key to your superlative success does not lie in "luck", but rather hard work.

This is why passion is so important. If you don't love what it is, and if you're not passionate about your work, your business will not be the most successful in the world. Any super business will have a leader driven with extraordinary passion. They are always thinking about the business, and they don't know what else to do. It is the only thing that brings them pleasure, and it is why they choose life over everything else.

The Force members are passionate people who inspire others to achieve their goals by sharing their passion.

3. It is important to build an inter-complementary staff - no matter how well-rounded, hard-working, or brilliant a leader you are, you cannot do it all by yourself. He also realizes that he can't always find the right team to help him reach his goal of achieving a high-level business. The Force is an essential part of this. This leader knows how motivate his team.

A great leader can work with any group they have. A leader with The Force is able and able to motivate all members of the team to try their best to make the business succeed. This leader recognizes the strengths of every member of the team, and uses them to make them feel valued.

Team members will be more willing to go the extra mile to fulfill the trust they have been given by their leader. Your team will perform at its best and be willing to work hard, which is what will make your company a leader in the world.

4. Allow everyone to be the owner of the business. A leader's greatest quality is his ability to inspire and motivate others. The Force makes it possible to transform motivation by making everyone feel like the owner of the company. Every person will do everything they can to promote the company when the business is theirs.

The Force will help you build a business that is people-oriented. This business is built ethically, values all its members and follows high moral standards. Each team member is expected to give their best and help the business meet its goals.

5. Suffering in spite of your weaknesses is a sign of success. While great leaders have talent, super leaders do not suffer from them. Super leaders are able to use negative input and transform it into great success. How is that possible? Force leaders stay grounded on the ground and don't let success take over their heads.

You will be amazed at the humility of each one these super leaders. They are humble and will not allow others to make the same mistake. They are polite, friendly, and willing to listen to suggestions, advice, and other points of view.

Their greatest strengths are their drawbacks, because they are what keep them humbled. These drawbacks remind them to be humble and not perfect. They also help them stay open-minded to learning new things, no matter where they might find them.

This is how the business will grow, because it does not rest on its sands. A great leader will never say "there's nothing you can teach me that I don't already know". Instead, they seek out other perspectives in order to discover new angles, new direction and new ways of doing business.

6. They are often the first to embrace changes - change scares, intimidates and terrorizes most people. These aren't super leaders. A super leader, a leader who is connected with The Force, welcomes change. He will be one of the first to embrace it and understand it.

Change is scary and difficult. Many businesses exhibit inertia in this sector. Super leaders can adapt to change. These leaders use innovation and research to stay ahead.

It is easy for leaders to distinguish themselves from those with The Force.

You can also see that these traits can all be learned and adapted to bring your business to the heights of your dreams.

The Society's Use of The Force

The Force is the combination and two super leadership factors: The Force is the combination of charisma and self-confidence. The Force is an innate ability that makes people successful in their professional and personal lives. The Force users will always be remembered as unique.

The Force is the ability to attract people wherever you go and do whatever you do. You'll instantly recognize who it is. These are people who make or break societies.

5 Ways You Can Use the Force To Be Popular In Your Society

How can they do this? What makes these people so special? How can we get there and be like these people. These are five aspects of The Force that make their bearers special.

1. You are visible - your presence is what makes you standout in a crowd and command respect. Imagine a king wearing regular clothes. Despite his simple clothes, his majestic posture would still make him distinctive. The same goes for a plain-clothed FBI agent or vice policeman. Their body language, how they move, and their manner are all indicators that they have been assigned to police duties.

The Force will make a person respectible, regardless of their appearance, location, or other activities. They are royal; they are extraordinary; by simply being there, they are the center point of attraction.

How does it happen? To project presence, it is essential to pay attention not only to your appearance but also to the details around you. To put it another way, you should appear effortless and natural.

If you're a lady, go natural with your makeup, natural tan, and natural hairstyles. The look should be flawless, but not overdone. If you are a guy, a military haircut will look great on you.

Two more things are essential, regardless of gender:

* A genuine, warm smile that puts people at ease.

* A commanding position (walking with your head raised, your back straight, and a balanced gait).

2. It is important to have proper mannerisms. A king may be rude or apathetic. Can a respectable person be loud, petty or abusive? The answer is no. A royal person will act as such. He will show humility while still displaying the correct mannerisms. For example, a man would be gallant towards a women. He will greet everyone with courtesy, no matter their status.

This person will show humility and kindness to others. The Force requires no proof. Their charisma speaks louder and more than words. People love their regal demeanors and mannerisms.

3. You have exceptional finesse. Although you might think right mannerisms, finesse and finesse are interchangeable terms. Finesse is the ability to control situations, instill trust and inspire people. To show finesse at such a level, you must practice these attributes:

* Do not rush or be hassled. This will result in losing control over the situation.

* You are patient when you see others making mistakes. You are prepared for every situation.

* You project confidence and control over the situation. Even when you feel scared, you don't let that show in your face. The Force makes it possible for super leaders to control their emotions, and even reign in their fears.

* You are sensitive in your actions. Loud actions belong to boorish people who are either superior or below others. Balance is always possible.

4. You are mysterious. Mystery, enigma, subtility are characteristics that spark the imaginations of people. People are attracted by the anticipation of what's next. This is a powerful feeling. People love this excitement as it is rare in everyday life. It makes people feel passionate and would like to be a part of your life. This is one characteristic that The Force people possess. These are some simple steps to learn how to be enigmatic.

* Always have some cards handy - no matter what your plan may be, it's best to keep them close at hand. Keep something only you know, that only only you can do.

* Be unpredictable. The Force is not a leader. The Force means that a super leader will act in an unpredictable manner. Because he thinks differently and acts differently than other people, this is why he is so unpredictable. A master chess player will know that you

need to plan at least 5-6 steps ahead. Keep them guessing.

5. Master diplomat: Diplomacy is an exceptional attribute that allows one to handle difficult situations and people without getting into conflict. Diplomacy demands that you master many social skills.

* Be a good listener. To make the other person feel comfortable, and get him to trust you, it is important to be a good listening partner. You must encourage the other person's self-expression and not just his.

* Genuine compliments are earned. Everyone loves compliments. If you give genuine compliments to someone, and not flattery, it will make them feel loved.

* Don't be too modest. Always show respect for others. A modest person is much more attractive that a pompous. Instead, pay attention to the traits of people around you.

* Keep your emotions under control - A person who has The Force will be able always to control his emotions, regardless of whether they are anger, joy or fear. The person you portray should always be seen as being in control of his/her situation.

* Develop a sense humor. There is nothing more attractive than someone who knows how to laugh at themselves. You must also be able smile and make people laugh. It might take some effort to instill a sense humor but it is well-worth the effort.

Chapter 6: Kaizen In Its Original Context Business

Kazien is a term used by self-improvement people and is very well-liked by all who want to be happier, better, richer, wiser, and healthier. The concept was initially a business term. This understanding can help us better grasp the concept and be able to apply it in our own lives.

If you own a business, all of this will be of benefit to you.

Kaizen is the Origin

Japanese for "improvement", "change for a better" The term kaizen can be translated as "improvement"/"change for the best". But, the term kaizen refers more to continuous improvement or small, incremental changes.

Kaizen had this meaning for the first time in business. This was especially relevant to the first methods of Toyota automobile manufacturer. The strategy was later successfully used in business, as well as self-improvement. The Toyota Way Book explains Kaizen and allows for its widespread adoption.

The self-improvement crowd has, however, allowed some creative license in how it uses Kaizen. Kaizen can be simplified in many ways by self-help literature, while others miss some key concepts.

Kaizen is all about getting down to the details. You can make small changes that will make a huge difference. This is not what the original meaning of the word means. Self-help books often say that it's about "flossing our teeth" every day to establish new habits.

This doesn't mean that this advice is not valid. While this book will address all types kaizen, it will not be exhaustive.

First, let us understand the strictest business interpretation. We will then move onto the "official" version. Which just so happens to be very powerful and often overlooked.

Types of Kaizen

Kaizen has been divided up into two terms in business.

* Flow Kaizen

* Kaizen Process

Flow Kaizen looks at the "value stream" in order to identify opportunities for improvement.

Consider a large production process that includes many steps. You might not think that every step will have a huge impact, but if you consider the whole process, even small changes can make a huge difference.

Process Kaizen is the "concentrated enhancement of a single proces." It is the process of improving one particular step at a time to make it better.

Kaizen is often described to be "bottom up," meaning that it starts at the foundation level and works its way up.

These are the changes that you can make. The floors can be cleaned to improve your business. Why? Because clean floors result in happier staff and fewer accidents. This makes it easier to store and retrieve information. That means happier customers and more cash left over. This leads to happier customers and higher morale.

Simplify your waste management and get rid of it

Kaizen, however, is about looking for ways to reduce waste.

There will always be "waste" in any given process that can be eliminated. These errors can often be eliminated, which will make your life easier.

This can increase the speed of a project. This can bring about huge and profound changes in a company.

Let's suppose that you write articles for a huge blog and then upload them every day to WordPress. WordPress is an internet publishing platform. Upload the article and add images, formatting like headers and bolding.

Your current workflow looks something like this:

* Write your article

* You should read through your writing and find typos

* You upload the article via WordPress

* You go through the work, upload images, and format it.

This approach is fine. Nothing, really. Except that you aren't using this method to your advantage. It's because you are currently going through everything twice. This is one to ensure that the spelling is correct and another to add images.

Why not?

* Write your article

* Upload it into WordPress

* Take a look at it and correct typos.

This effectively merges two steps into just one step. It may take slightly longer, but it will be much faster than doing each separately. This could potentially save you considerable time and effort.

Let's say that you save 10 minutes each article and upload 10 articles every day. This is 100 minutes more than you would have needed. Perhaps this will allow you to upload an extra article. In this case, you may be able to make an additional $30 per hour.

Kaizen might be a good option for sole traders looking to make an additional income.

$30 per Day without increasing your rates, working more hard, or changing anything about the business

Kaizen is unabated. Because there is likely still waste.

What if you could eliminate the uploading time by writing directly to WordPress? You could also combine your formatting and proofreading together. Could this save you time?

Kaizen continuously searches for ways to cut waste and streamline flow and improve processes.

Here are some examples for "waste", which a Kaizen practitioner might seek out in a business.

* Defects - Poor copies, mistakes, errors

* Excessive Processing - Repairs

* Overproduction - Overestimating demand

* Waiting: Waiting for the next part of the chain to become available

* Inventory - Waiting on stock/supplies/materials

* Transportation: Time spent transporting persons or goods

* Moving = Excessive movement of people or machines

* Non-utilized talent: Using skilled workers to fill a need in a less-skilled area

While it may seem less applicable to your everyday life, this type is actually quite powerful if you consider your own processes.

Kaizen Concepts To Consider

Kaizen gains even greater power when you consider other concepts that can be applied to your business. These are force multipliers as well as automation. This is also true for our personal lives. We'll see more in the future.

Force multipliers: Any tool that makes it possible to do more with less effort or time is called a force multiplier. For example, a hammer allows you to hammer a lot more nails than you can with your fist. You can also consider a force multiplier in your business a computer, or any piece of software. The same applies to a forklift truck which allows one employee significantly more pallets.

If used properly, these can save you lots of money and help to increase your output. Josh Kauffman (personal MBA author) explains both the benefits and importance force-multipliers but also points out their potential dangers and downsides. A force multiplier not only increases your production, but also magnifies the risks and potential errors. Kaizen is vital. A more efficient system will result in a more scalable system. It is crucial to build your business correctly from the beginning, so that it can continue growing.

Think of it as throwing a basketball. A ball that has a slight deviation in trajectory is unlikely to hit its target. A slight deviation of just a fraction over a considerable distance is a big deal.

Thinking in terms a force multiplier allows us to potentially increase productivity, output and overhead without increasing time or overhead. Ask yourself whether it is possible to implement a system that allows the same team members to accomplish more and faster than they currently have.

Automation: Automating any aspect of your company's business processes, including marketing or production, is automation. This is the logical next step from force multiplication. Automation will often involve using software or a machine to make something, with little to no interaction from humans. There is a high risk of making an error by automating. You need to be more vigilant and watchful.

A good strategy when looking to expand your operations is to find ways to automate aspects. A smart businessman/woman should always look for ways of making themselves obsolete. That means looking to the future. This can not only increase your output but also allow you to create a service. What can you do to offer a service that eliminates the need for humans?

WordPress is a perfect example. Matt Mullenweg

crew succeeded in automating the process to build a site and make it a product.

The 5S of Kaizen

Kaizen can be described as five words. 5S is a form of business shorthand.

So what are 5S? They are:

Seiri/Sorting refers to the ability to organize your work and keep it in one place.

Systematic Arrangement or Seiton: This refers to how you arrange your items so they can be easily retrieved. This is essential for storage businesses and logistics, and it's also important for valet parking.

Seiso/Shining refers to cleaning all equipment and the work environment. This can reduce mistakes further down the line.

Seiketsu/Standardizing: This means using standard processes that can be repeated, tested, and fixed.

Shitsuke/Sustaining. This means you need to keep adhering to the previous S.

This system was originally developed for manufacturing. It can still be used in all aspects of your daily life.

Kaikaku, the Opposite of Kaizen

Kaizen has many benefits, but is not always the best fit for every situation. Sometimes a process, or flow, is too complicated. Kaikaku, which is a drastic change, is the right response in these cases.

As you may have guessed this means to abandon the old processes and start over. These kinds of major changes are often met with immense psychological resistance. It's important to keep your mind on the right things and not indulge in nostalgia or sentimentality.

That is to say, if a website you have worked on for 5+ years doesn't seem to be gaining any traction then it may be time to completely rethink its strategy.

Failures will sink you more quickly than you can keep them going. It is crucial to know when it's kaikaku and when kaizen.

Kaizen for Fitness and Health: Kaizen for Kaizen

We have seen quite a few theories regarding kaizen. We've seen how it works at work and in manufacturing, but now it is time for us to look at it in action - to see how it could work in our lives.

We begin by looking at Kaizen when it applies to working out.

Microworkouts

One way to implement the principle of "small, everyday changes" to improve your health and exercise is to employ the "microworkout." You will be doing a very short workout each day. This gives you many benefits, including the ability to workout less stressfully, a lower effort level and the possibility of developing a new fitness routine.

Let's imagine that you are going to the gym four days a week, but instead of eating 500 more calories per day, your commitment is to do 20 pressups every morning.

It's clear that you're getting some exercise each day. It will keep your blood pumping at the minimum, and it will tone your muscles slightly.

Plus, you will form a new habit.

FUN FACT - Many people believe that it takes 30 day to form new habits. But, recent research suggests that it actually takes closer 66 days. Philippa Leal, a researcher published in the European Journal of Social Psychology reviewed the habits of 96 participants over 12 weeks. Each person tried a new habit for 12 weeks, and each day reported whether they had succeeded with their new habit. The analysis of the data revealed that it took 66 consecutive days for successful new habits to form. However, this was highly dependent upon each individual. In some cases it took between 18-254 and 254 days to form the new habit.

It doesn't really matter how long this takes. However, once you've been practicing a particular behavior for enough time - say 66 consecutive days - it becomes easier to build on that. Now, you can do 20 push ups every morning. It is easier to go from this to someone who does fifty press ups in a morning than to try for 50.

The same goes for other beverages. Once you get used to drinking 50 fewer calories, it might be easier than ever to stop eating other calories.

True Kaizen & Getting into Shape

So is this really kaizen?

Not really.

The microworkout has definite value. There are also benefits to cutting calories.

Kaizen for health and fitness means to look at all your activities and identify what's making you sick.

This is a great place to start. It might be worth looking at other ways you can reduce your caloric intake.

You might also look for reasons that may be keeping you from training properly or eating right. In other words, you are going to view your entire lifestyle as one large "flow"/ "process" and then try to make improvements.

You are trying to get into shape but don't know how to motivate yourself. The problem with this is not psychological, it's physical. How do you break bad habits, and how can you get in the gym even if you have reservations?

First, let's assess the psychological and other situational factors that may be preventing you achieving your goals. After that, let's look at ways to eliminate them.

This will be great for your health, but it will also work in other areas of the life.

Remember that energy is finite, just like time. You cannot continue adding more tasks to your day and expect to see results. You're likely tired and maybe even depressed. That's why you aren't in shape.

If you are looking to improve the health of your family, it is important to consider ways to make your daily life easier so that you can have more chances to improve your health.

You can make powerful changes to improve fitness

What Can Go

Begin by asking yourself "what can be cut?" If you are currently burning all of your energy at the end of each day/week, look at your daily routine and see what you can eliminate. This could be as simple as deciding to stop going out on Sundays. You may need to organize your thoughts: Maybe you could talk to your employer and ask about working from home a day a week. This could make you save huge amounts of time and energy.

Even small things, like getting a dishwasher for plates to be washed again, can really save you energy and allow you to spend your time exercising.

Don't try to add more to you life. Ask yourself what can be cut.

Where to fit it in?

We can save hours and even money by switching the order for uploading articles. The same holds true for exercise.

Ask yourself this question: When is the best hour to exercise? Take into account factors such as showering. Do your workouts in the morning before you take a shower?

Or, you could find that working out at work during lunch breaks is more convenient than traveling.

Again, we want to reduce "waste", either in the form or movement of "non-utilized potential" (that's us!).).

More small fixes

However, there are likely to be other small changes that you can make to this efficient mindset. You might be surprised at how many calories your body is burning per day. It could be that you are not moving enough in a given day like many people. This can easily be highlighted by wearing a fitness watch or stepping counter.

If you sit at your computer all day and don't get out of bed in the morning, you're unlikely to lose weight. Your body won't adapt to an active lifestyle.

You can look at the current routine and identify ways to improve it through small exercises. It could mean walking to the bus stops or taking the stairs.

Being able to leave a stop earlier is an option. It might be a standing desk that allows you to check your email, or it could be a gentle walk after work.

These small changes make a difference and force your body to adapt. Your day will look identical if the movement is integrated into it in logical ways.

Takeaway

The bottom line is: If you aren't in good shape right now, this could be due to a stressful and too busy lifestyle. This indicates that your lifestyle might be inefficient. There are probably things you can do now to get back energy, time, or vigor.

At the minimum, you will be able to find more efficient ways to accommodate the new items that you are interested in.

This is a far better way to get in shape.

Kaizen Personal Finance

Personal finance is one area where the kaizen approach works well. You can make your life richer by using the kaizen strategy and fixing your personal spending.

That doesn't mean you need to cut out all your lattes.).

The first step is to accurately and thoughtfully create a budget. This will reflect your cash situation and the amount you want/need to save/spend.

Create a Budget that is More Effective

Let me say, every year, or every few month, you make a budget. This budget is what you hope will help to keep you on track with your finances. You decide how much food, gift, and entertainment you'll spend, and then you make a concerted effort to stay within these limits.

This is probably fine for the first few day, but then unexpected expenses catch up with you and quickly add up. Before you

You're not even aware that you forgot about your budget. And by the end, you're spending just as much as usual.

Don't worry, you aren't unusual. You're just like most everyone else on Earth. But that doesn't make it a problem. It's something you have to work on. These tips will help you make a budget you'll actually stick with.

Monitor and Improve

Last time that you wrote down how much money you could spend on food, did you just jot this number down? This is what most people do. Surprisingly it doesn't work. If you want to make a budget work, then you have to focus on the how. That means keeping track of your spending and then looking at how much money you can spend. Not just assume you'll spend $20 less every week shopping. But think about other ways to do it - like buying milk at lower prices or going out for dinner only once a week.

It's important that you work toward a goal instead of just making random statements about your spending habits. This will allow to you evaluate your accounts honestly and make smart choices in order achieve your goal. You will almost always find small things you can do to improve your finances.

It is possible to reduce your spending and make big improvements, but this will not be possible if you don't have a concrete picture of your income or outgoings.

Plan for the Unexpected

Problem with budgets is that they can't help you if your rail card gets lost and you need to replace it, or if you loose a tenner. A buffer of $20 is a good way to deal with these "unexpected", (you should be able to anticipate them by now). In reality, you can easily calculate how much you are losing to "unexpected" losses over time. Then you can take an average of that number.

Limit Your Cash Flow

To stop yourself from spending excessively, limit the amount that is going into your existing account. Spend money only from the account you are paid into. Instead of setting up a standing-order to have a set amount of your pay package transferred to another account. The account will not have an excess fund that you can use for shopping or other purposes. This will only cover your budget. You can also keep the money you need for next month. Your card will stop working if you go beyond the budget.

This is an example in automation. You can automate the transfer from one bank account to another. Make mistakes, though, and automation is powerful. This is why it's important to perfect your personal financial system before automating any transfers.

Give Rewards

How do you improve your budgeting skills when you save money towards something? This effect can be duplicated throughout the year by offering yourself rewards for budgeting well. You might offer a gadget you like, and then tell your bank that you need to save a certain amount before you can get it. This will help you be more motivated to stick with your budget. The best part about money is the fun you can have with it!

Use Apps

Pro Tip. There are many apps that let you see the spending of all your accounts simultaneously and then give smart, actionable guidance. This can come in handy when you have to track spending across multiple accounts and cards. One good example is Emma for iOS (https://emma-app.com/). This app lets you see how much you spend across the major banks, creditors, and breaks it down into smaller amounts.

Useful categories include personal care (eating out), charity, business, etc. PayPal is even included. This can be incredibly useful to quickly set realistic targets and identify areas for micro improvements!

You'll see quickly where most of your money goes and can add restrictions. Also, you'll know when your budget is not being met.

Takeaway

Kaizen refers to making small and easy changes to your life. The key part is to be smart about the process: being able to accurately track your spending and then making small changes that will have an impact on your finances. Kaizen is about efficiency.

Chapter 7: Kaizen For Productivity, Business And Productivity

Kaizen was designed originally for use in manufacturing. As such, it makes sense that Kaizen is a perfect tool for increasing productivity in your company and improving efficiency.

Instead of giving you a list with specific changes to make here (which will not be the case for everyone reading this), I will rather outline a method for assessing your current workflow and making improvements.

Find the Important Points

The goal is to free up time and energy for your most productive day. Begin by writing down all the tasks that are completed every day. This list should include everything you do every day, such as booting up the computer and organizing files.

You will then evaluate the duration of each block of activity, and whether or otherwise it could be performed faster.

Simply by making your computer run a bit faster, you could save yourself 10 minutes every day.

This means that you will spend almost an entire hour each week making tea. Making tea can easily take 15 minutes per day, which adds up quickly to about one and a-quarter hours each week.

Once you've identified the issues, the next step is finding ways to make each one faster or more efficient. These are just a few of the ways you can make your day more enjoyable.

Sticking to Your New Rules, Avoiding Errors by Using Checklists or Flow Charts

But how do we ensure these new productivity rules are maintained? How can you ensure that errors and mistakes do not creep in, which will take more time? One solution is to use flow charts and checklists.

One study on the effectiveness of nurses and doctors showed that doctors are far less likely (than surgeons) to make serious mistakes when given a checklist. This idea was rejected by many doctors at first. Doctors saw it as being "checked up on" and continuously monitored even though they were able to work independently. Even experienced doctors make fewer mistakes by following precise checklists. This forced them into paying more attention to the finer details.

Flowcharts have the exact same power. A flowchart can be used to quickly describe a situation and determine the best course for action to obtain the desired result.

A manager or business owner may often act as a flowchart and a checklist. Staff will approach them with problems or challenges, and they will give them solutions and checklists to follow.

This basically means that the boss can organize their business better and be removed from the workflow simply by using flow charts and checklists.

Flow Diagrams for Problem Solving

In a car shop, this is one example of how it could work. If you were running an auto repair service, you might often use a mental flow map to diagnose and solve problems. If you were to ask the question, "Does this vehicle have 'X" problem?" Is it making "Y" noises? Is it a N' model and make?

This can be done by creating a flow diagram that will allow less experienced staff to arrive at the same conclusions. Similar to checklists, checklists will help them avoid small mistakes while they work on the problem.

This will allow you to get more questions answered and make it easier for you to work on the business, not in it. This will allow you to ensure that every customer gets the same level of attention and great treatment, from beginning to end.

What if your flowcharts and checklists don't do the job?

Then you can look into how to fix the problem. Otherwise, you will be much less stressed and your company will run smoothly.

Biohacks, Life Hacks, and Biohacks

Kaizen is best when it is inspired by the idea of "life hack" or "biohack". This is small lifestyle and health changes that can have a huge impact on your life.

Some biohacks may be absurd. They promise the universe but deliver very little. Lifehacks, which look amazing on Instagram but aren't practical in real life, can be the same. So, our goal is to search for the ones that do work and then to incorporate them into daily life. You will do better in every aspect of your life if it feels good.

Temperature could be key to good night's sleep

As we have known, ambient light plays a major role in determining our quality sleep. So, by using many devices that emit blue light we're actually upsetting the 'external Zeitgebers' (external signals) and destroying our body clocks. Native tribes do not have such issues and therefore sleep better as nature intended.

Recent research found that the sleep patterns of these indigenous humans were quite different. They slept much later than others, often staying awake until the wee hours of the morning and not allowing the daylight in to reset their biological clocks.

What set these rhythms? It's interesting to note that one thing they had in common was that they began waking up when temperatures rose. In summary, this is a crucial cue in regards to sleep quality. Thermostats can be used to remove this critical element.

Take-away from this? It might be the most effective way to improve your sleep. This will help you feel better and allow you to do more.

How to Wake Up on Time Everytime

The best thing you can do for your life is to get up every morning at a reasonable hour. By getting up 30 min earlier you can save 3.5 hours of your week for exercise, learning, and reading.

Naturally, we need sleep. Therefore, the goal here is not to get less sleep by sleeping 30 minutes longer. It is more about getting rid of the time we waste on "snooze"

Some of the advice I will give you is not what you might have seen elsewhere. But don't forget to stay with us.

The key is to not pick up your mobile phone until the alarm rings. Instead, spend some time looking at it. Many experts will tell your that picking up your mobile phone will affect your hormone levels and cause you to be reactive. If you do not turn off notifications and stop checking email, your phone won't make you reactive. Bright screens encourage cortisol production, which aids in waking up. The best part is that it can also be used to help you get up.

Why? We're addicted to our phones. Therefore, the emotional pull to reach them is strong enough that it can outweigh serious tiredness. It is even more important if you have something to look forward to.

However, the act of looking at your phone can help you get out of bed. Even if you only take one small step, you will find it enough to get you up and moving on.

Your alarm will go off 15 min before you get up. The alarm will sound when you wake up. Once it sounds, get out your phone or tablet and read some news. In just 15 minutes, your morning will be up and running.

The Best Supplements

Supplements can provide important support for your health. Does it really hold true that your diet can provide everything you need? Sure! But, most of us do not. To be safe, it's sometimes safer to pop a Pill.

These types of supplements are natural substances that should be included in our diets. Substances proven to improve alertness, energy level, and overall wellbeing.

You'll notice an increase in energy and focus, a decrease in flu symptoms, better sleep, and a greater likelihood of getting sick. You'll notice that this will help you in all other activities. It's an easy change that makes all future change easier.

This is a simple and effective supplement that can dramatically improve your mood, brain function, and energy levels.

* Vitamin D – Taken every morning

* Omega 3

* Magnesium Thireonate - Taken in the evening

* Ashwagandha

* Inositol

* Creatine

* Lutein

* Curcumine

Inspiration Hacks

Do you ever feel lacking inspiration? Do you ever feel deprived of inspiration?

Inspiration is a highly valued and abstract commodity. There are several ways you can increase your inspiration. Listening is the first.

Audio books can be used while you're doing chores and going for walks. This allows you to focus your brain and, if you find the book interesting, it will make you more creative and focussed.

Watching junk on TV and browsing Facebook is a big mistake. This ineffective content leaves us feeling less productive and useful. You should choose carefully what focus you wish to place your time on.

Dress to Impress

It is an easy life hack that can have big repercussions on how you feel about yourself and others.

If you're not comfortable in clothes that you can wear around the house, you'll be less productive and less likely to do useful work. In addition, others won't treat and respect you as a professional.

Smart clothes will make it easier to be productive and more focused. You will find that people are more willing to work with and for you. This is one example of "wasting" time (by spending more time getting ready), that ends up being an investment over the long term. Kaizen isn't about pruning.

Intermittent Fasting

Intermittent fasting offers many benefits. It can help with weight loss and may even lead to life-extension through autophagy. Additionally, it improves energy and focus and saves time when preparing breakfast.

Finding balance

Kaizen is about increasing efficiency and optimizing your lifestyle and workflow to achieve more. This can be a great way to approach your life but it also has its limitations. Your goal is to maximize your lifestyle, but you may end up missing out on the simple things that make life worthwhile, like snoozing on the sofa with your spouse, or binge-watching junk TV.

Consider going out with friends for drinks.

These kinds of waste should be completely eliminated, according to self-help books. You should grind and grind until you get what you want.

We disagree. We disagree. Kaizen needs to be balanced to function.

Input & Output

If your only focus on work, you'll lose inspiration. As an 'input/output' device, think about yourself. The act of watching movies and playing video games isn't a waste. It's an outlet for creativity and inspiration. If you work only in output, you will eventually lose your inspiration and creative juices.

It's the reason I always do my best when I return after a few weeks off.

Spending time with others and relaxing are also important ways to recharge. Your energy can be a finite resource.

It's a valuable skill to cultivate. It is important to have'soft skills'. You can get along well with anyone and make friends easily. You must be able to switch off and is a vital survival skill.

Keep your positive attitude!

A positive attitude, persistence, and self confidence are three of the most important qualities that an entrepreneur, athlete, or other person working toward a long-term vision can have. You must be capable

To take your lumps in the event that things don't turn out as you had hoped. And to be able and willing to jump right back on that horse.

It's much easier to stay positive if you have a large circle of friends and family you love and trust.

You are encouraged to be optimistic and courageous to try again. How much happier do you feel after a good day with friends. These kinds of experiences are the foundation of life. They're also nourishing for the soul.

A setback in your business or training can cause you to lose your entire life. You might even give up.

Make the Most Out of Now

This may sound a little strange, but it's true. You never know what you might find. You might not live to see the fruits of all your labor. So, it is possible you won't live the life you want or have the chance to rebuild those relationships.

The irony of it all is that most people wouldn't live a lifestyle full of decadence and relaxation. I love to write and learn and train and I hope never to retire. We find happiness when we are able to do what we love.

balance. To achieve a goal, we need to have a purpose. While the journey can be more exciting than the destination, spending time with family and friends, or taking the time to read a good book will help us keep our feet on the ground.

The truth is that most of us will try to attain some obscure concept of'success,' so much so that our happiness can be lost. In reality, traditional success can often make it harder to spend more time with friends or follow your passions.

It's likely that you have lots to be proud. You will never be satisfied if your life isn't lived to its fullest. Your success will be less meaningful.

You can feel good about eating whatever you want, no matter how small. Whatever productivity "gurus" may tell you.

This is as vital to your mission and as important as the mission itself.

Chapter 8: Structure Of Personality

Before we start to discuss how we can measure the personality of another person, we will first need to consider everything that makes up that particular personality. Part of our personality is formed from the DNA we mentioned last chapter. You also have all the genes that make up your body, so don't be too concerned. But that's just the beginning. Your physical body can become a work of art with a little effort. It can also be turned into a useless lump of blubber, if you don't treat it well. It's easy enough to imagine how you could move from one condition to another depending on how you treat your genetically programmed body. You can change the DNA factory settings that have created your personality so far. We want to know what your personality is outside of the DNA factory settings.

Habits

You can only control the habits that you make. Habits can also have an impact on your personality. Habits are things you do repeatedly enough to become second-nature. We can slowly reprogram ourselves as individuals. For instance, you may have a bad habit of dropping f bombs every four to five words. Or, you may have a habit that makes your friends laugh when they start discussing politics. You may also be prone to sighing loudly if a single person in your office starts speaking up at meetings. We all have habits that we are aware of. Some habits are totally subconscious. We'd be horrified to hear someone suggest that we do something that is as bothersome as the one who does it, but everyone hates. Egads!

Memories

These words will also affect our personality in very unpredictable and strange ways. As you are reading these words, you may be thinking about them. Based on the sentence about bad habits, you may have conjured up memories. What memories do carrots bring back? What memories do they bring back of playing on a slide in a playground or other outdoor activities? What memories do we associate with being caught outside in the rain? We have many memories. The problem is not so much with the actual memories. The issue is usually how we use those memories. How we react to these memories is a key factor in how we feel about ourself. Some memories we might believe are awful memories, but are in fact a strong indicator that we are truly suck. As soon as we suspect we may be recalling those memories we get those terrible "I suck!" thoughts. feelings. And if your thoughts are dominated by "I suck!" You will notice a difference in your non-verbal behavior and personality if you have negative memories or thoughts. We'll discover later how to use our memories in different situations and also how to go back into the past to rewrite them as many times as we want. While the content of the memories will remain unchanged, you have the ability to change your feelings about those memories. This is something which you can easily do all on your own. It is also very powerful. Most people believe they have little control over their memory. We may believe we can control our memories. But most people think they cannot suppress the memories that cause them pain. We'll find out why this is similar to trying and cure athlete's heel with a flaming shovel. Very dangerous!

Preferences

We are all goal-driven organisms. We are social animals. Social interaction is a great way to get our needs met. The way we choose to interact with others is an important part of our personality. All of us have an assortment of instincts that drive our behavior. We all like to eat. These preferences impact how we eat. The people we choose to live with, our physical type and what neighborhood we would like to be a part of, all have an impact on how we feel about ourselves. It is part of our personality that we seek intellectual stimulation. But how we choose and satisfy that need is another.

Meta Programs

These filters are filters and are a shorthand way to organize preferences. Your motivation strategy is your common metaprogramme. We all are motivated by two things. The goal is to get away from pain and towards pleasure. Each thing we do has two goals: to move away, now, or into the future, or to make it more pleasant, either now, or in our future. Every individual has a different preference in how much pain is enough to motivate them or how much pleasure can be expected to help them move forward. It is a common myth that people who are more motivated by getting away from pain are less likely to be in the best of life. They are only motivated if they feel like they will be consumed by doom. Once they are no longer in control of their lives, they will lose their motivation to get back on track. This type person is constantly being harassed and hounded by their landlord to pay rent. They are also about to lose their job, their car is late (they need to hide it from the repo men), their life is in peril, but somehow they stay on the right side of the storm. The other person, the stereotypical one who is motivated only by big dreams, are the inventors who start large companies but need multiple assistants for the small details. These are big dreamers who have high aspirations and are unable to settle for the ordinary things (relationships). While their plans seem to be in shambles, it doesn't seem that this bothers them. Meta programs that you use to receive validation (from yourself or from others) are also common. What is your ability to see new things? No matter whether you're a big picture guy or a detail person.

Both short-term as long-term intentions

Your future goals will affect your personality. You will behave differently when you're relaxing and having fun than when you rush to finish a report.

Social Reference Group

Each person is different. Some people are socially outgoing with close friends, but they are more reserved with strangers. They're all the same regardless who they're around.

Recent Experiences

It is possible to have a unique personality if you are the one who has just lost in the world series. Your personality may be very different if you've just won a $50,000 prize in a competition. Many people have a unique personality when they're young, hungry, and another when they're old and successful. We love fiction because it shows us the characters' personalities changing slowly. Movies with no character growth are regarded as unrealistic and boring. Motion pictures, books, and TV series with strong characters who have fascinating character arcs are more compelling than others. It is possible to imagine that strong characters in fiction are a result of our desire to experience personal growth in our own lives. Fictional characters are subject to many circumstances that force them to change. It is our desire to be forced on a journey that will change our personality for the better that makes this story so compelling. There is an old saying, "Hard times make hard men." Hard men are the best. Good times make softmen. Soft men make hard times. The cycle keeps going. The good news is that just like we can consciously make changes to our body's health through exercise directed, so can we consciously make improvements to our personality. There is no need to wait for difficult times to force us.

Outer Game

You can seperate a personality into 2 sides. The outside, or exterior. It is what can be seen or observed. This is also known as the outer game. This is the portion that everyone else perceives. This is where you will find the attraction. There are many clever metaphors we could use. One example of a clever metaphor is the one where a chicken makes another egg. The possibilities are endless when you consider the long history of chickens, eggs, and other animals that you have. An egg can be a chicken's way to make another chicken, or an egg can be a bird's way to make another egg. This is the second view, which comes from the point of view that humans see DNA shells as helping DNA to make a copy. Personality can be seen in a structure that is somewhat similar to it, but which is also quite abstract. Our inner games are made up of our thoughts. Our inner game helps us satisfy our inner desires. The fulfillment of our inner desires is what we aim for as humans. Our inner game influences our outer. Our inner game influences our targets' inner games. In turn, their outer games affect their inner game. Which in turn leads to what we want. This four-part view shows us how human interaction between two individuals. We are lucky that our inner and external game can influence how they respond to us. That is our sole purpose. To create an attractive personality which essentially works on its own. This allows us to just show up, relax, and attract whatever we like. Attract multiple candidates and then pick from among them according our needs.

Outer Game Behavior

You can put a lot of your inner game into non-verbal behavior. How we move in social situations. How tall and straightened we stand. How fast and how slow we move. How quickly or slowly our heads turn. How often do we swivel around our heads while looking around. How much we use our gestures.

Where we place our drink, cigarettes or other social props.

Outer Game Face Expressions

Our facial expressions are different than our general behavior. People who are interested can learn a lot from our eyes. One piece of evidence is how quickly your eyes move (or not) around the room. How long you can keep or break eye contact during conversations. How you keep eye contact during conversations can make the difference between selling or rejection. Just pointing your eye at another person is not enough. If you stare at someone with fearful eyes, they will be quick to run. You will get the opposite effect if the person you are looking at is kind, gentle, or has soft eyes. Your mouth and the way that you hold it when relaxed can also reflect your inner state. Basic body language classes will help you spot a fake and real smile. Real smiles show real happiness. This is because the muscles around our eyes are involved. Fake smiles that show nothing are only made up of the muscles surrounding the mouth.

Outer Game Speech

Most people think about outer games when they think about communication. They are specifically thinking of proper word order and proper words. If you have ever seen Harry Potter or read the books, you will know that the wizards spend a lot studying the magic spells. They must be able to speak the correct words in the right sequence with the appropriate energy. Otherwise they will fail. Anyone who has ever read a beginner's guide about sales or seduction will know that the best words are all that is needed. Online forums devoted to selling and seduction are filled with a lot of words. How to say. When to say. What should they say, what to say and how to do it. Humans place great importance on what they say, but less on their actions and other behavior. Later, we will see why the words we actually say aren't nearly as important than the rest our outer game, mostly the nonverbal communication.

All Outer Game Should Be Objective

If you're ever confused about the inner game and the outer, (we'll devote the next chapter to the definitions of inner games), then imagine that anything falling under the outer gaming category is something you could watch and point out on video. Any technical advance you require is acceptable, so long that they can't read the mind. With a sufficient amount of video tools, for example you could record the exact angles and movements of the entire body, as well the facial muscles. Audio equipment could be used for measuring the exact tonality of speech, the space between words, and speed of speech. Imagine yourself as an alien race studying Earthlings. Imagine you have an invisible and silent drone camera, which can follow people around the world and record them at different angles. You can then use this invisible camera to monitor every tiny movement or sound in your ship.

Homework

While streaming services are the best, this works best. You can still use YouTube or any other video site for free. View any scene from TV or movies where people interact socially. It doesn't matter if the person is famous or not. Watch scenes from TV shows and movies you've never seen. Then, observe how they behave and what makes them attractive. Look at their faces and their movements. They move fast or slowly. Don't attempt to guess their emotional state. Just try to classify them as attractive or non-attractive. This will allow you to choose whether you would like them to interact with you. This is not possible if you are not influenced by the physical attraction of their bodies. Try to think in terms only of social and general attraction and not romance or sexual. Keep this going for a few more minutes each morning over the next few day. It is important to identify the characteristics of the outer game that you find attractive.

Inner Game

Inner game drives the outer world. There are some outer games that are reflexive. The inner game, however, is instinctive. We can nevertheless say that every outer behavior is determined by the inner state. Any combination of emotional emotions or instinctive wants can be described as an emotional state. Hunger is a common instinct. Eating is an outer behaviour. Combining our deep instinctive desire to eat with other long-term plans can help us make better decisions about our outer behavior. Already, we can see the complex relationship between inner game and outer behaviour. Here are the main categories or ideas that make our inner game. It is clear that it will be harder to measure the inner game and define our inner one.

Inner Game Beliefs

These are an overused and vague term. Beliefs describe the way we view broad concepts. If you believe that the world has unfairness, it is a belief. The belief is possible to express in nearly endless ways. The world is unfair simply means that two people can work the exact same amount of effort and produce different results. A world that is unfair can mean that it may be very difficult to find the motivation and perseverance to keep trying. It is possible to find something good in the world if it happens that we receive something that we did not achieve. Many people won't waste their time trying to find the owner a 100-dollar bill. It would be easy to conclude that we are lucky to have found a hundred-dollar note, while the person who lost it might think it means the world has unfairly treated him. These beliefs are also a way to see yourself and the world around you, including how you view strategies for getting what you want. You might find yourself working in low-wage work and having negative views about money. Beliefs could be generalized opinions about how you think about certain topics. It is not common to have the lifestyle of a rockstar, easy money, or sex that we dream of, but it is possible. Although many people share the same outer-game, non-rockstar lifestyle, there may be different inner-game beliefs. You can choose to identify beliefs as positive or supportive of your need, or negative or very restrictive in regards to meeting your needs. There are two types of beliefs: subconscious beliefs and conscious beliefs. Negative and subconscious beliefs are the ones that can cause self-sabotage.

Confidence

This is very much like beliefs. This is similar to beliefs. You might be confident you can make a delicious grilled cheesy, but that could also affect your outer game. An example of two people making a grilled cheesy would be enough to show you your inner game grilled cheese making skills. With very specific activities we can see how confidence levels impact outer games behaviors. These assumptions can also be made about both. If we observe someone making a grill cheese with their outer game skills, we naturally assume that they also have inner game confidence. Given their many successes in making grilled cheeses, it is reasonable to believe that their confidence comes from these experiences. If your goal was only to get a decent sandwich of grilled chicken, you have two choices: one with grill cheese confidence or one with grill cheese anxiety. He keeps checking the heat and lifting the sandwich to check for doneness. Naturally we would choose the one who has the highest level confidence in grilled cheese. Many previous successes are a sign of inner confidence. Strong outer games indicate a strong inner game. This example is too simplistic and silly to show how intuition can help us choose the inner game confident people who will have high chances of success. If we wanted to compare this process with an AI robot that is self-aware, then we could say we just feel the confident grilled Cheese maker has the best chance of making a good product. If we look at the confident grilled chees maker, this "feeling", or attraction, could be described as a positive feeling. Our AI friend might conclude, "Evolution has given us this intuition to quickly sort for others that have a high probability" of helping us find success."

Future Visions

It is possible to describe our inner game by saying that it is dependent on what we want for the future. We are, in essence, goal-seeking organisms. Our bodies are constantly in search of a unmet need. Even if our only activities are eating and sleeping, we are all in the same process: consuming and digestion, which then leads to elimination. More long-term goals that are well-planned and consciously chosen will influence our decision making in every day. People who have long-term and strong plans tend to think differently and thus act differently from people with fewer plans.

Memories of the Past

When we are thinking about the future we often check our past performance and our strategies. In order to make our decisions more confidently, we need to avoid making mistakes. Doing something that has been associated with success will give us a sense comfort, familiarity and positive expectation of success. This will have an effect on our behavior. Imagine two people walking into an unfamiliar social situation. One will be comfortable and familiar with it, the other won't.

Inner Game Reveals Inner Game

This is not an easy thought to think of. But, the concept of a skilled and confident grill cheese maker can be extended to any situation. We are always looking for ways to satisfy our customers' unmet expectations. Sometimes this means a grilled sandwich. Sometimes it's just a friendly chat. These unmet desires can sometimes be very specific and targetted, while other times they may be vague and general. People who show the outer-game behavior that gives us an intuition about our chances of success will make it easy for us to feel attracted or happy. The outer game behavior of people who have a low chance for success (e.g. It is unlikely that we will be able meet all our needs with these people. They won't create that feeling of attraction. The same way that our intuition can differentiate a well-known grilled cheese chef from a novice cook, so can we sort for positive, attractive social interactions. Everyone can have that same positive vibe. We can even sort through a room quickly to identify those people. You radiate your inner state by what you do. This cannot ever be switched off. This is exactly why professional poker players use sunglasses and baseball caps to disguise their non-verbal communication.

Homework and People Watching

Find somewhere you can relax and take in the sights of others. Imagine you are an alien in human body and are studying the human race. Sort people into two categories. The first category includes people with weak inner games. This could be due to lack or familiarity with their surroundings, lack in confidence and lack of expectation. The second category is people with positive inner gaming, which includes confidence and positive beliefs, expectations, and attitudes about their surroundings. This might seem odd or unethical since you are directly judging people. It is important to remember that this two-way information flow is always available and being measured. It's not strange to try to make this conscious. Simply observe, categorize and categorize the inner game. This should be done independently of their physical attractiveness. The attraction to someone who is extremely physically attractive can lead you to believe that they have a positive inner game. Do not practice with someone who is attractive or of the exact same gender to avoid this.

Attractive Personality traits

Let's talk about some positive personality characteristics. This is not a complete list. But, this will allow you to be more attractive.

Social Intelligence

This is the ability to read body languages, understand what isn't being spoken, and discern when people are attracted or not confidently expressing themselves. Social intelligence will improve your inner game by allowing you to more accurately understand what is happening inside others' heads. Social intelligence isn't always attractive. Social intelligence is when we use inappropriate language, aren't able to know when to stop, and don't want to go anywhere for longer than necessary, this is a sign of a lack.

Confidence

Your confidence will make your appearance more appealing. Confidence, like playing the keyboard, is situational. It can also be used in general situations, such as when dealing with strangers. Both words are synonymous. A strong positive belief in your ability to succeed in any situation is key. The most attractive personality trait you can acquire is the belief that you will succeed. You don't want to be unsure.

Solid Frame

A solid frame can be closely linked with confidence. A frame is a measure of how strong you believe you can make your intentions manifest in any given situation. A strong frame can be one of the most powerful tools you have to create a persona.

Long Term Results

Your personality will shine if you have a strong, long-term goal or set. If you aren't clear on your career goals, or what you want to do in the future, you will be less appealing than someone who has strong career goals.

Short Term Outcome

Your personality will shine if you have a strong, short-term outcome. Being able to achieve a strong, short-term outcome is a key component of a strong frame.

Are you open to receiving assistance?

People who are open and willing to help people in real need tend to be more attractive to others than those who do not. It doesn't necessarily mean that you should be offering advice to everyone. An attractive personality will have a strong sense to help others when combined with an intelligent social mind.

This will be greatly appreciated if there is no obligation to offer help, or even waiting for an obvious thanked. You are able to use social intelligence to spot someone in genuine need, offer and give any needed assistance, and then quickly remove them.

Contact us for help

It is also important to recognize when you have a need for help. It is important to ask for help when you need it. This will make your attractive. Our society has many instincts. You must ask for help and be open to helping others. You can ask for help or give help when necessary. These two behaviors make you highly valuable members of any social circle and are therefore highly attractive.

Highlight the strengths of others

Recognizing the strengths and honesty of others is a sign of appreciation. No one will forget what it means to be acknowledged, either through words and/or through helping others. We all want recognition for the valuable contributions we make. You'll be attractive for any talents or special skills that you can identify in others.

Validate Other

Validation can be used to identify positive traits or skills in others. However, validation can also refer to highlighting them. Validation may be used to recognize accomplishments, grievances as well, injustices that have been suffered, and any other emotionally significant event. Validating someone else sends a strong message to them that you see and appreciate them. In many stories, the strongest binding force between two characters is when one of them sees the other. If you can validate something about someone else, it will have a strong effect on them. This trait can be extremely attractive when it is combined with high social intelligence.

Creative

A valued person will be able to think outside the box and come up with innovative solutions, suggestions or ideas. Your attractiveness is greatly enhanced by your ability to think creatively, make creative comments, offer creative solutions to problems, and give creative compliments.

Lead/Follow if appropriate

If you are a leader and everyone wants it, you will be an example to others. Attractive qualities include allowing others the opportunity to lead and supporting them as they become better leaders.

Authentic

It is possible to be authentic and still be attractive. Genuineness and positivity will help you be authentic. True to your nature and being authentic can make you a serial killer. But, this wouldn't make it attractive. Many cult leaders proved to be very attractive because they were genuine. A combination of many of these characteristics, along with genuine authenticity, is the best combination. This can be broken down into more categories.

Congruent and authentic

Congruence simply means being true to yourself. Nearly all adults avoid expressing certain feelings or energy. Only babies are truly compatible. When they're happy, they share it with everyone. They are happy when they feel sad, angry or frustrated and let everyone know.

Honesty, Genuineness

It is possible for someone to act sincere. This skill is well-known among politicians, sociopaths, and A list actors. But, it is desirable to have honesty and congruence in everyday interactions. This is as long as you aren't a cult leader and/or a serial killer.

Appropriate - Genuine

It's not possible to keep your congruence honest and appropriate without hurting many feelings. If you were congruent, completely honest, without worrying about being proper, you might tell a stranger that you don't like their hairstyle. One of the most common jokes about fictional AI characters is their inappropriateness. They will say things that sound authentic, consistent and true but are completely untrue.

Calibration

All of these traits are based solely on an attractive personality. One of the most attractive traits that will benefit all of these traits is the concept of calibration. This term is used loosely in various forums and message boards. We'll need to clarify it. It refers originally to calibrating equipment. You might wonder how you could be certain that your electronic thermometer measured the correct temperature. You can calibrate the thermometer against a known temperature. One way is to place it in a saucepan of boiling water. Called calibration, the process of changing an instrument to match a measurement (usually over several measurements with several different values) in order to calibrate it. Calibrating people is possible in the exact same way. Take your time to get to know them and their communication style. This is closely tied to social intelligence. Social intelligence is more observational. Calibration, on the other hand, uses social intelligence to analyze or understand nonverbal communication. It is possible to have friends or a couple who are highly calibrated. This means that they know a lot of what each other feels without using verbal cues. Although it's not something people do consciously, calibrating can be taught. You'll be more attractive if others can calibrate you. We all have the ability to calibrate other people. However, as we age, our social fears can cause us to lose that ability. It is something we need to rediscover rather than learning from scratch.

Chapter 9: Human Behavior

We will be discussing the basic principles of human interactions, and the factors that drive human behavior, in our next chapters. It is important that we understand the fundamental operating procedures of humans in order to make better decisions. It's easy, without giving human behavior much thought and consideration, to fall into a luck trap. This is where those with high social success are fortunate while those who aren't are unlucky. Even if social success is a given, it's easy to feel like the results are not within your control. However, once you understand the concepts below, you'll feel much more in charge of your personality and the results which you can achieve within any social setting. Two people can be likened to two cars. The first person has no idea what the car does, and is even unable to explain why it needs gas. They view the car as a mystery. If it works, then it does. They have no control over how their car operates. The second person knows cars and car maintenance much more than adding gas when it is needed. They are knowledgeable about car maintenance, including engine maintenance. They can control the vehicle's behavior and quality.

Goal seeking organizations

Humans are inherently goal-oriented. Once upon time, there wasn't life on Earth. Then, life appeared. This unique life could both take in material and use it in a variety of ways. The first was to use that external material as building material. The second option was to make that material energy-friendly so the lifeform could move about. Sometimes, moving was limited to growth if the organism is a plant. Some movement could be described as actual movement. This means that the animal can slither across the ground or jump off it. All life evolved from this simple and ancient form of life. We need to survive. To do this, we must be driven to obtain things beyond our control or to move to safe areas. These are our instincts. These instincts are what drive us to want things that we don't own. In any given moment, right now and until your last breath, you'll have many unmet instinctive wishes. The food you eat is moving through your body from the moment you swallow it to the point you throw it away. Every step of this process is incomplete. Many processes are going through various stages of completion within your body. Your relationship to your immediate world is continually moving through various stages of completeness. It is impossible to live without a number of unmet goals, or desired outcome, conscious or subconscious. It is impossible that you live without being working towards achieving several goals. We are all living entities that are constantly striving for an outcome. We are always working towards achieving outcomes. These may be called desires, needs or goals but in essence they all have the exact same basic structure. There is something you don't possess and something you need. You must take responsibility for your environment to ensure that you create that outcome. Sometimes, all it takes is a simple shift in our sleep. An unconscious, automatic behavior. Sometimes this is a very conscious behavior that requires a lot thought.

Everything comes with a price

Each effort to achieve an end result costs something. Sometimes that something is not much more than a few calories. These costs may include money, time or risk and emotional discomfort. Every time we (or the lowest and most basic lifeform) desire an outcome, it's necessary to expend some effort in order for that outcome to be achieved. To have energy we must use some energy (even just for chewing).

Positive ROI is crucial

ROI can be defined as return on investment. This is typically a business term. You can get a 100% return on your investment if you spend $100 per day advertising your business. You can spend 100 and get back 200. Even though we don't consider monetary costs when making decisions, our instincts dictate that actions should only be considered if they will bring in a positive return. If our ancestors had been accustomed to spending two thousand calories in order to get only one thousand calories, they would have gone to their graves. The constraints of a negative ROI must be adhered to by even the smallest living organisms. Any living thing which continuously uses more energy than what it takes in will die very soon.

Emotional ROI Important

This principle also applies to our emotions. Positive feelings are preferable to negative ones. Feel good about eating food with usable calories. It isn't good to eat foods that aren't usable calories (such dirt and tree bark). It's not good. To determine if our ROI is positive or negative, we can use our emotional feelings to help us gauge how happy we are. Hunger is a bad feeling. It is an indication that you need more calories. Fear is a bad feeling. This is an indicator that danger is near. Happy relationships with good people are a great feeling. Evolution has programmed our brains with emotions that are often correlated to survival value of the things we associate them with. The feeling of eating delicious food, even when you're hungry, is very satisfying. Feeling sexually and emotionally connected to a partner is great. It's essential to human survival that we have strong human relationships. If you consider ROI, it is easier to focus on calories and money. The same rules apply to emotions. We will only do what we think is best for us. The long filter of nature has made it possible for us to associate good feelings, which are more likely to ensure our survival, with things we like. Similar to natural selection, we also have evolved to associate harmful feelings with things that threaten our survival.

Modern World can create confusing feelings

However, it's important to realize that our instincts as well as all our feelings were developed way back when we lived in a much simpler society. The easiest example is hunger. In the past, food was scarce. Our hunger must be strong. To avoid forgetting to eat, our hunger must be more than the food available. This doesn't seem to work in today's world. This results in the opposite. This is the opposite of what makes a strong sense. The positive trait of being totally submissive to hunger was an old one. It is very difficult today to ignore hunger as we are constantly surrounded by food. Many people are overweight, which is a natural consequence. As the clock ticks, the higher the proportion of overweight people, the wealthier a society becomes.

All emotions are today confused. But, there's one thing that remains constant. If we believe we will have a positive ROI on our emotional investments, then we won't do much. Everyone has the exact same problems. We are governed and guided by our need for positive energy and emotional ROI. But, our primitive instincts view of the world has made it very confusing.

Human Interactions

The same rules apply when we humans interact and communicate with other human beings. We won't be involved in any way with another human unless our belief is that we will get better. We can think of our state before we interact. Then imagine what happens after the interaction. If we believe that the interaction will provide a net benefit, we will allow it to proceed. Of course, we don't know this. This is akin to hunger and having sex. Our survival instincts are built into our brains. It doesn't take much to figure out how many calories you need to provide energy. We just think about what we like to eat, and then we eat. Our subconscious will decide that interacting with another person will be a net positive and we feel a positive when we do this. This is conscious when we look at buying something. This can be seen through a barter lens and then applied to money.

Basic Trade

If you're a child who has a backpack lunch, you might be able to swap with another child. One possibility is that you have a banana and prefer an apple. It's easy to find someone who prefers a banana over an apple. This is usually very simple. The trade is easy and pleasant as both parties will get a net personal benefit. Imagine you are enjoying your banana. You get five points of pleasure. Think about eating an Apple. You get ten pleasure points. You then find another child who has the opposite set. They can imagine an apple with five values and a banana with ten. You trade, which only costs you a quick conversation. Each of you get five additional points of enjoyment. This is why it feels great to trade with other children. You get more pleasure for both of you, and it feels great.

Collaborations

This may seem silly, but keep going with it. Let's assume you are a student at school. You come across a candy machine that sells candy only for a dollar. You only have fifty cents. Find another child with fiftyc and who is willing to buy and give you a candy bar. This is sort of like trade. Your fifty cents won't get you much if you do it all by yourself. However, if you are able to find a partner, it is possible to get something for fifty cents. While you wanted to trade your fiftycents for candy, the trade was impossible. The good news is that you can now trade once you have joined forces. After you had formed a coalition of like-minded people, you could each get fifty cents worth or candy.

Human Social Animal

This sounds simple but is an essential part of human social behavior. It is a good feeling to trade with other people. It feels good when we work together to get things we could not get on our terms. Humans are highly social beings. We evolved to be able to trade, and to pool our resources. Trading is both financially and emotionally rewarding. The process of trading is pleasant and enjoyable. This tittfor-tat behavior is seen in many animals. We both enjoy trading pleasure for enjoyment, but we also enjoy doing something together which we would not be able do on our own.

Consciousness, Unconscious and Intuition

Trade and collaboration exist both consciously, and unconsciously. The conscious decision to have an apple was made when you saw you had a banana. This was followed by the conscious decision that you would stand up, go around and speak to as many people as possible in order to find a trade partner. You made the request for collaboration when you met a trading companion and presented the offer. The other kid thought about the matter and concluded that a trade would make sense. This was driven by an expectation for a positive emotional outcome. Sometimes trades are instinctive and unconscious. When you wander around a meetmarket for instance, you may have come across someone who was equally attracted to both of you. The following thoughts were common amongst the two of you:

Perhaps they would make a good partner to have children. You might have enough in common life goals and interests to make raising children together a positive, rewarding experience.

What's more? You are right. Those that made it comfortable to keep eye contact. Those ancient instincts that made it feel good to get to learn more about that person. This is a great feeling, especially when it happens naturally. It's perhaps the most wonderful feeling we can ever experience. It must. Because human children are expensive to raise, it is essential that parents have strong emotional bonds. Take into account that the best way to get to know someone is through eating. It's wonderful to share a meal with someone you love and are slowly falling in for. It has been since time began, and it will continue until all humans are alive.

Halo Effect Explained

Now, we can understand the reasons for the halo effect. As we look out on the world, all of us have created criteria to find the perfect partner to help keep the human race alive. Contrary modern thought, these criteria do not require any effort. It is the first thing that we see about a person's physical attractiveness. The more physical attraction we have, the more our deep instincts tell us that we should get to know this person. We feel strongly about a person when we see them. In a very basic and non-political way, our instincts determine which person is the most attractive. The people that our instincts deem the most physically attractive make us want to know more. But this does not mean that we will have sex everywhere we go. Their physical attraction is the first step in that direction. Their actions will all be given some subconscious, benefit of their doubt. The first step is purely about physical attraction. All the next steps are personality-based. These personality-based criteria can be more flexible if you are physically attracted to them (often subconsciously).

If they're attractive enough to our sexual instincts, we can give them credit for many first stage personality criteria. This is the halo phenomenon. These people will find the things they say and do more valuable than someone who is less physically attractive. But this only works in a very limited way. In other words, the more that we have to get involved with them and the more that any mutual outcome is dependent upon them, the harder it will be to filter them through personality filters.

Studies have shown that short-term relationships with men can be difficult for men. Their partners should be attractive but that's all. They should consider their personality and physical appearance when selecting long-term partners. Although the halo effect may be strong and very real, this only applies to short-term relationships. To develop an attractive and strong personality, you must go beyond short-term relations and interpersonal relationships.

Highly valued people

We're now going to tell you why all those positive traits that we talked about a few chapters before will make it more appealing. Understanding the reason will make it easier for you to comprehend. Knowing the functions and needs of a car is similar to knowing how to take good care of it. Once you know why those traits are so important, you'll be able identify the traits that you want to exude in each situation. Additionally, you'll know which traits are beneficial so you can make changes. It's a lot like looking at the fuel gauge for gas. You don't need to be conscious to see it. These may even seem instinctively desirable. It's like a caveman meeting another and asking if they should fight until the end, run away, or join forces.

The Long Term and the Short Term

We will explain them very vaguely to make it easy for you to imagine them in extreme cases. One is as a business partnership. And one as a casual conversation with anyone you happen to meet. Both will follow the same basic rules.

Mutual Goals

Partnerships are mutually beneficial when you both want the exact same thing. As humans, we feel more at ease working with others or as a team than trying to do something on our own. No matter your goal, whether it's to get to the bus stop and build the next tech company worth billions of dollar, it's much more enjoyable to work with someone who is trying to achieve the exact same thing. Nearly always, humans can achieve much more together than they can independently. Even if you share your fifty dollars with a stranger kid, working in groups is more beneficial than working alone.

Strong Personality Traits

Someone who exhibits many of the personality traits described above will send a strong positive signal. This will inspire others to be positive. Even if your goals are not urgent, people who display these personality traits have positive partner energy. We all know that it is impossible to predict the future. This is true now, as it will be thousands of many years into the future. And it was true thousands and thousands of year ago. These traits have led to a strong desire in us all to find partners with those who exhibit them. These traits send a message to their deep instincts about you as someone who will help them get what they want. And you will be thankful for their help in getting the things you want.

We love giving and receiving advice

It is great to give advice. It can feel so good, in fact, that we often give way more advice than we should. While it can feel imposing to get unasked for help, good advice is a blessing. Most people feel that they are not in control of their situation. Most people wish that someone could tell them exactly what to do. Sharing that burden with someone is the best option. Being able to share the burden of not being able to decide but still trying is as great as having someone carry your heavy load. You might learn something new about the bus schedule by having a conversation at the stop. This could help you save money and time. A business partner who is starting a new tech company may have ideas (based upon your ideas) that are different from what you would have imagined. It is possible that the caveman you met on a hunt might be from a different tribe than your tribe. They may catch fish, but your tribe hunts for deer. This might result in a long trading relationship. You are often given credit for the creation. Everybody has a deep instinct that suggests it is better to seek counsel from others, even if they don't know much. It's just as important to listen to the advice and get help of others as to give your own advice. Everybody has an instinct that tells them to look for new friends and partners.

Be and Bring Out the Best

As we all have many goals to achieve and more that we need to meet, it only makes sense to have better friends, colleagues, and collaborators. If you are just having a random conversation, being someone who naturally brings out your best will make it much more fun and lively. Your chances of business success will be increased if your business partner is the best. Your chances of getting along a great caveman or meeting his charming sister and killing a mastodon might go up. Your personality trait of bringing out your best will make it easier to attract others.

Leaning and Being Led

Leaders are vital for groups. The leaders of a group need followers. A group can succeed with a leader and followers who are strong. Maximizing the success of the group and each member's success is possible only if they feel comfortable following along, if necessary.

Everyone Wants Somebody

Everyone has a number of unmet basic needs. They are organized into a hierarchy in our brains. Each of us have a particular thing we desire more than others at any given point in time. Sometimes this is food or drink. Sometimes this is the touch or voice of a friend. Sometimes this is a friendly conversation between a friendly person in friendly social environments. We all like being helped getting our needs met. We all enjoy helping others achieve their goals. Being attractive simply means having the personality traits that will enhance your success as well as their success, should there be any friendships or partnerships. Attractive personalities are a strong indicator that you will help them achieve success. This will appear as an overwhelming emotional feeling. You will become stronger the more they know.

Homework

Keep an eye on people, and try to find attractive personalities through this mutual cooperation. The future will hold many tasks. Think of complex tasks. Imagine yourself being the star in some of your favourite action movies. Based only on who they are, what kind of people would you want to join your team? A group is a key element in many thrillers and adventure films. Rarely is there one hero. Nearly all stories have a team consisting of several people. Each person has their unique personality traits. Do you think of yourself as a fictional character? What character types are you able to identify when trying to find attractive people? Although it might seem silly to compare your personality with fictional characters, they are actually based on the type of personalities that we love. These characters are actually simplified representations of real human desires.

Form and Function

One of the most important ideas is the relation between form, function and form. This will make you feel like you're in the chicken/egg relationship. It doesn't matter where you live, the other side can be found. Chickens are entities using eggs to make more chickens. Eggs refer to entities that use chickens in order to produce more eggs. It's similar to a good old T-shirt. They can be worn inside or outside and still look great. It works both ways.

Form and function

This is a slippery concept. Both terms are closely related. We'll start by defining each term. We will then examine all the ways in which one can become the other, as well as vice versa. It will help us decide where to start. It is true that improving one will improve the others (like chickens or eggs), but overall we want to find the best solution. They have roads in the United States that cars can drive on. There are spaces where pedestrians can safely cross streets without being made into pancakes. This is a very important idea. One way to designate these walk-across-the-street safety zones is by drawing a couple of lines with white paint. This will signal to everyone that this is a safe area where pedestrians can cross the street. This funny example is meant to demonstrate the difference between form & function. Because of their function, cross walks are commonly called in the United States. Their purpose is to make pedestrians safe from the other side. In Australia, they're not named after the function; they're named after the form. What they look. They are called "zebra crossings" in Australia. In reality, the name is a mix between form and function. The function is represented by the part that crosses, but the part that zebras is the form of it is what it looks. It looks as if someone has painted zebra stripes on it. American ears understand a zebra-crossing to be where zebras cross streets. But that sounds silly unless one is driving across Africa.

Japanese Enjoy Twice the Food

Japanese food is well-known for the attention they place on its appearance. That means they want the form (how it looks), to be as enjoyable as the food's function. It is important to look at the food before you can enjoy it. The plate's form is beautiful, as well as the arrangement. When you finish it, you will enjoy it again. The actual taste and nutrition you need to be healthy. However, there may have been times when you were not concerned about how food looked or tasted. One the other hand, it could be that you have been to very fancy and expensive restaurants where the function (not only how the food tasted but also how many calories it required) was poor, but the form of the food (the way it looked on a plate) was spectacular.

Human Form & Function

It is difficult for humans to distinguish between form and function. This is confusing for us humans. More confusing than zebra crossings or beautiful food on a expensive plate. An example: Putting on a costly shirt makes you look better, so it's a function thing. A nice-looking shirt can be a form thing. However, if you wear it to a club you will get positive attention. You are viewed as a confident person by others. In any given situation function flows from form, and form flows from form.

Simple Form and Function

Smile when you are happy. This is both form and function. It's an expression of your inner state, which others can also see. It is also an expression your inner state. Function can be referred to as it. Functional happiness is possible. This applies in both directions. You can start by feeling happy inside your brain. This shows up on your skin. Because your brain is connected with your face, it also moves in the opposite direction. This is what you can do for yourself. When you are feeling negative or neutral, smile and pretend you are happy. You will eventually start to think happy thoughts. However, function and form can seem a little too complicated when it comes down to humans so we will use a more understandable label.

Inner Game & Outer Game

Instead of thinking in terms if form and function are important (which is too loose when you think in terms human emotions and behavior), instead we will be focusing on inner game as well as outer game. You can think of inner game as everything that you feel. Your emotions, your thoughts and your self-talk are all things that inner game can help you experience. Our definition of outer games is everything you expose to the world. If you were an alien disguised here to study humankind, outer would be the only thing that you could observe. Everything else would have be inferred. Some things will be quite easy. If you see people laughing and smiling, that is a sign they are happy inside. If you were to look at the top poker players, you'd have no idea who they were thinking. For the remainder of the guide, we will be focusing either on aspects of inner games or aspects of outside game.

Two Sides to The Same Coin

But you can't just change one thing without changing the others. Sometimes, one can make a quick change in your outer game by showing others. This will cause you to shift quickly to your inner world (what you feel on the inside). This is called the fake it to make it strategy. This applies to things like smiling while giving a speech and pretending confident. This means that if your smile is faked happy, it will make you happy inside. But, as you probably know, there are many more things than smiling. Some things are better if they go in one direction. Certain things are better changed from an exterior game standpoint while other things are better from an interior game standpoint. This makes it even more complicated because there isn't an all-inclusive strategy. Everybody's experiences and memories are different. Everybody is unique. A one-size-fits all strategy might work well for someone, but not for everyone. This is your job. You must understand the process. This is not something that everyone can discuss, as everyone has a different inner-game experience. For some people, such as those with a limited inner game experience, they only need to improve their outer game. For them, the importance of inner game is greater than that of outer game. Others may be able to get more from addressing inner game issues. To them, inner games are more important than outer games. When we say "more important", we mean it's more important to concentrate on and work on. You don't have to do anything unless it works perfectly. It's up for you to decide which one is more significant (which requires more focus or attention) in which circumstance.

Inner Game Exercises

One of the biggest myths about self-development in any field is that inner problems aren't as difficult to solve as outer ones. Our body is what we pay attention to. Skills, endurance, and other things are important. We are intuitively aware that it takes time for people to change. It's not easy to lose weight. (Many people still fall for the latest "lose weight without effort" diets. However, if we consider any kind of inner problem, we feel it should happen faster. Most of us believe that the best way to succeed is by accepting new ideas into your head. As though understanding a new idea will magically change your emotions, memories, beliefs, etc. Many people believe that everything in the self development industry is bogus. Snake oil is absurd. Imagine being an alien who lived among humans. Your job was study the self-help business. You might have spent several years reading everything, from the most renowned seminars and techniques to the best books and gurus. It might be worth measuring the difference between before and afterwards to find out which methods worked. This could be useful for both diets as well as sports programs. It is possible to take a look at all of the people who use financial self-help. Since you were an alien, you could look at the financial lives for everyone before and after they ate the self-help stuff. You'd probably find that most people were worse off after using the financial selfhelp material. There may be a direct relationship between the cost and how much you were able to get the self-help material. Further research will reveal that financial self-help material has the greatest financial effect on most financial matters. This is also true for dating courses. Or general personal development courses. You'd be able to conclude that most selfdevelopment is hooey. However, you could try this alien-scientific theory to all your weight loss efforts. The result would be very interesting. Most people who consume self-help information about weight loss will not lose weight. They actually gain just as much weight throughout their lives than people who don't consume any weight loss material. This would be extremely puzzling. It would be possible to bring all of the weight reduction material into your alien research laboratory and conclude that it should perform. Then, you'll come to a surprising conclusion. But, the techniques work only if people apply them consistently. If you start to observe people who do go to the gym, then it might be worthwhile. You might also take a look at what people eat. Then, you'd find that people who lose weight or keep it off follow the advice in weight loss selfdevelopment courses. This would prompt you to reconsider all non-physical selfdevelopment such as financial, relationship, and communication. This is where your problem lies. All health and physical issues would require things you could measure. Outer game items. What they do. How often they exercise. What they consume. However, everything else (financials as well communication and relationships, etc. The rest of the world is largely dependent on inner game stuff. These are the things that an alien cannot measure. But, you may be surprised to learn the interesting truth. The inner game stuff is as hard to master as the outer. The gym won't transform your body, but you can change your outlook on life. For your body to change, you need to do the exercises every day. This is not a time limit. You should aim for an hour a day. At least three days a semaine

Game secrets for the inner game

This is a hidden secret, but not one of those "as long as you know this secret everything's going be super easy !!!"". secrets. This secret is the difference between success & failure. You will also save tons of money if this is something you really want. You can't change any inner game issue by using a technique. It is all about the consistency. These techniques are straightforward. They are just as important as any form of exercise. So many people waste money on selfhelp. They come up with a new idea. They develop the new idea. They think they have a new idea. But then nothing happens. They believe they need another idea. So they decide to purchase another course that will teach them another idea. They are enthused by the new idea. But, nothing happens. They are soon spending a lot of time and money to learn these new ideas. These new ideas are a great experience. As they learn the latest ideas from the most renowned gurus in the field, they are surrounded with hundreds of screaming people shouting at them. Then they go back home and nothing happens. Imagine what you would learn about physical training if that was how it worked. You are reading a book with great promises about your amazing future. One of the central ideas in that book was to do a different type of situp. Now you do that one different situp. You then looked in the mirror to see that it didn't work. You should probably learn about another ...". This is exactly how people approach any type of inner game work. They will do it once, perhaps twice, and then they'll go looking for a new method. Because being bored is boring. (Like doing situps). It is enjoyable to learn about things, especially if you are surrounded by screaming fans, gurus, and famous people.

Inner Game Practice Techniques

The remainder of this guide will cover powerful inner-game practice techniques. Some will require purposely recalling and deliberately remembering memories. Some involve watching people while having a specific goal in mind. It can be hard to hold onto a particular idea. It's akin to sitting ups. Situps can be difficult at first. However, if you do ten of these every morning, you'll soon be capable of doing twenty. Then, thirty. Then fifty. And then, one hundred. Then it's a couple of hundred. Inner game exercises can be done in the exact same way. They are difficult at first. You will struggle to do them for long. If you practice them consistently, they will strengthen you. These will make a huge difference in your inner world, if you keep practicing them long enough.

A Hot Body Is Good

If you worked out for an hour every day and realized that you don't enjoy eating, you'd be pretty pleased with your body. It would be possible to have a beautiful body. You could even become a professional models. The halo effect is important. It's really not that deep. You'll find that people will be more interested in tangible things once they get over your awesomeness. This is what they will be learning. This is what you will be gaining if you don't do any physical exercise. In fact, let's do a mental comparison. A gorgeous woman with a beautiful body and an average personality. The average person with a flabby physique but a remarkable personality. A world class personality will allow you to be in more relationships, gain more real social status and communication skills that can help you navigate any situation. It takes only a gorgeous face and a great body to be able smile your way into or out of any situation. You'll be a rockstar soon if the effort you put into your body's health is just as important as it is for you to be healthy. ...)

Outer Game Exercises

How do you determine when you should practice the outer game exercises When they're easy. If you have ever tried to do any outer game stuff but are unable to concentrate, that is an indication you should be doing more inner work. That's totally fine. Attractiveness is a worthwhile goal that merits a lifetime of effort. The majority of exercisers recognize that physical activity is an integral part their lives. Also, you should try inner game exercises. These inner game exercises will help you conquer planet Earth. You may feel like the slowest kid in math school, but don't be discouraged if you feel that you are doing more inner work than others. Most people's energy is spent outside pretending they are happy, while inside they are filled with unwanted emotions. As you build your power, let them keep faking it. This article will cover some of the ways you can make your inner game more powerful.

General Movements

This is something that you should immediately start to do. Walking without thinking is common for most of us. Therefore, how we walk can reflect our inner world. World class criminals know this. They can see pedestrians and pick out victims just by looking at their bodies. This is exactly how lions choose their victims and decide who to eat. They choose the weakest. They select the weakest. They aren't being cruel, this is part of their instinctive programming that maximizes their lion ROI. It's easier to kill weak animals than strong ones, so you get the highest return (meat). Criminals have the exact same situation. They want to get the maximum return (the highest amount of money taken from a target) for the lowest investment. An individual with a strong sense is more likely to be self-aware than someone with a weaker self-image. We'll talk more about exercises and details later. But for now, think of people watching to pretend that you are a criminal. Who would your mugshot be? Who would it be that you wouldn't mug for?

Eye Movements, Eye Contact

It is a powerful indicator of inner game force to maintain eye contact. Our brains are large due to the fact that we need so many brains in order to process all the visual information. Although our brains and noses communicate more strongly, the nose is only able to measure. It doesn't project information to others (unless it is trained to track the micro movements ...).of their noses). Eyes are, however, the window to the heart. Eyeballs include not only the eyeballs but also all the tiny muscles, and the kajillion combinations that muscles can make and emotions they represent. It is important to remember that eye contact is very powerful, necessary, but delicate. Even though you may be a complete mess, you can still go about your day like a boss. You can't pretend to be confident with the eyes if your inner self isn't in control. It is important to supplement any practice with eye contact in outer games with inner game work.

Verbal communication

Another thing that shows a fine balance between inner- and outer game is this. Take a look at our discussion about A list actors. Because it is so difficult to fake inner confidence with words and tone, the reason A-list actors get paid so well is that they can't be trusted. Your inner game condition will always reflect on how you communicate. The good news is that verbal communication can be practiced alone, unlike eye contact, where you need to communicate with another human. It is possible to imitate your outer game by using verbal communication. This is more effective if you're practicing for a speech. A speech that is authentically reflects your inner game strength will be more effective if there are other people involved.

Mental Focus

Active listening is an essential element in a strong personality. Passive listening, however, is not difficult. Just sit still, pay attention to the noises around you, and don't forget to open your ears to them. Being active requires mental focus, mental concentration, as well mental creativity. It's one to listen and understand the words of others, but it's another to be able to identify what is important, what isn't, or which emotions they have. It takes work to get to this point. Creative ideas are what make the money. Sometimes this will simply be offering advice. Sometimes, it may be sharing a story from your own experience. Sometimes, it will be telling statistics so they don't feel so alone. Sometimes they may be teased and made fun of. This is an inner game that's more important than the outer game.

However, it is possible to make this inner game into an outer one.

True Congruence

True congruence can be described as a complete transparency of inner game and external game. True congruence exists only in babies. Every bit of inner-game data they encounter is immediately translated into their outer game expressions. Congruence can be dangerous for babies as they get older. This is mostly due to negative feedback. With congruence, humans are taught to think "better safe than sorry". This is a very rare trait in adults. True congruence rarely exists between best friends or long-term partners. There are ideas and emotions that we all share with others.

Attractive Personas are the ultimate objective

The goal here is to be in a state where you can make the conscious decision to be totally compatible or not. This is called a "horizon goal", meaning that it's something you work toward. You might feel congruence in some situations. In other cases, you may not. However, this is the direction you want to take for the rest. To continue, you can use the inner and outer games to release any unconscious fear of true congruence.

Congruence is appropriate

Use inner game expressions to guide your outer game behaviours. Sometimes you'll want a strong response and other times, you might need to take a step back. How well you can read the situation (socialintelligence) will influence how much congruence you choose. When you know how to calibrate targets, congruence can be used for maximum effect in a particular situation. It might sound overwhelming. This skill is unparalleled. The ability to transform inner game emotions into outer games behaviors. A base level, like all skills is our starting point. Then, we improve and learn more. Then we move up to a higher place, where our unconscious performance rises. As an example, you might start off as a horrible tennis player. You might be awful the first day on court. But you can get better with practice. Playing against other players of the same level as yourself will make it easier to forget about thinking. The more you practice, your playing ability will increase without you having to think. This will also help you improve your personality. Now you know what your basic state is. The real you. As you practice inner and exterior game exercises (of which you will need to have social intelligence or calibration), you will slowly increase your natural, true self. Sometimes you will need to stretch and use more conscious thinking than normal. It's like playing tennis with a much better opponent, who requires more mental focus. The attraction level of the real self, who is a person who acts naturally, without thinking, will increase as you practice and get better. Just as it's always the true you playing and enjoying, it will always remain the true you showing your inner and outside game skills.

www.ingramcontent.com/pod-product-compliance
Lightning Source LLC
Chambersburg PA
CBHW060222030426
42335CB00014B/1310